W9-AEB-103

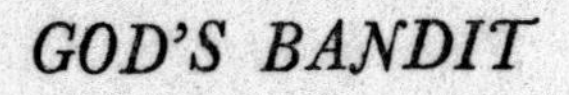
GOD'S BANDIT

Books by Douglas Hyde

I BELIEVED

THE ANSWER TO COMMUNISM

RED STAR VERSUS THE CROSS (with Francis Dufay)

ONE FRONT ACROSS THE WORLD

THE MIND BEHIND NEW CHINA

Don Orione, "Father of the Poor"

GOD'S BANDIT

The Story of Don Orione
"Father of the Poor"

by

Douglas Hyde

THE NEWMAN PRESS
Westminster, Maryland

— 1957 —

B
0

Nihil Obstat

JOANNES M. T. BARTON, S.T.D., L.S.S.
CENSOR DEPUTATUS

Imprimatur

E. MORROGH BERNARD
VICARIUS GENERALIS

Westmonasterii, die 6a Maii, 1957

FIRST PUBLISHED AUGUST 1957
REPRINTED JANUARY 1958

Printed in Great Britain for The Newman Press, by
The Windmill Press, Kingswood, Surrey

Acknowledgments

The author wishes to acknowledge his indebtedness to Ignazio Silone for help and encouragement given and for suggesting the title of the book; to Fr Paul Bidone of the Sons of Divine Providence, who was for weeks his interpreter, general help and good travelling companion; and to Fr Francis Hamer, S.J., for reading the proofs.

Contents

Prologue

In a stone-flagged refectory in the cellar of a technical school in Venice my supper of bread, gruyère cheese and red wine was brought to me one night by the old doorman. But he was clearly no ordinary doorman. As he spread my food and drink before me on the rough trestle-table he kept up a steady flow of conversation in a rich bass voice, backed up by a wealth of expressive gesture. He was short and stocky with an enormously broad chest made still broader by a great expanse of spotless white shirt-front.

"With a chest like that you should have been an opera-singer," I told him banteringly.

"I was, Signor, once," he replied. "That was my great ambition when I was a boy. When I grew to be a young man I found that God had given me a good voice, so my dream was realised and I went into opera. Then the most wonderful thing that can possibly happen to any opera-singer happened to me: I was asked to go to the Scala in Milan. I am a Milanese and it seemed the greatest honour that could ever be paid me. I was given solo parts in some of the best-known operas. Like this . . ." He threw back his head, expanded his chest, and a great torrent of music came tumbling out of his mouth and went echoing round the corridors of the empty school above us.

"You can still sing. Why are you here?" I asked him. "Why did you leave the Scala?"

His answer fitted into a pattern with which I was beginning to grow familiar.

"One night I was coming away from the opera house. Don Orione happened to be passing at that moment. He spoke to me, and I knew as soon as he spoke that I would follow him to the ends of the earth. I can't tell you why. He told me about his work. 'Is there anything I can do to help?' I asked him. He told me he wanted someone to do all the odd jobs at a school for street-boys which had just come into his hands in Venice—this school. I told him I would be the one. I travelled down with him to Venice and I never went back to the Scala as a singer again."

★

It was after midnight when I arrived in Milan and so, when I reached the Piccolo Cottolengo di Don Orione, I got quickly to bed without even bothering to learn the lay-out of the building or to discover just what was the work done there.

Next morning I set out to find a bathroom, and promptly got lost in a maze of corridors. Suddenly a door just in front of me flew open, and a legless boy, with a rollerskate-like contraption fixed to his seat, shot across the corridor in front of my feet, crashed open the door on the other side of the passage and disappeared into what was obviously the bathroom. The door through which he had come remained open, revealing a long dormitory in which armless and legless teen-age boys were climbing out of bed.

I had at one and the same time learned the whereabouts of the bathroom and also the nature of the establishment. It was one of Don Orione's six homes for war-mutilated children.

Later, when I set out to explore the building, I met the congregation coming away from Mass in a chapel which was buried in the depths of the great establishment. It was no ordinary congregation, for it reflected the many-sidedness of the work done there. There were old crones, deformed young girls, blind, senile and half-wit women, war-injured children, orphans. As I went down the corridor with this small army of the despised and rejected, I passed bright rooms in which were tiny lunatic girls, little human animals, and others in which lay bed-ridden incontinent old women.

Under the same great roof were 200 *mutilatini* (mutilated children), 100 orphan girls, 50 girls who were either mentally defective (some of them congenital idiots), crippled or deformed, 100 women suffering from mental disorders, 200 old women, either sick, senile or bed-ridden: 600 people whom no one else wanted to bother with. They were cared for by members of the Sons of Divine Providence and the Little Missionary Sisters of Charity, two of the orders founded by Don Orione.

*

Mayor La Pira of Florence is both lovable and unconventional. He is first citizen of one of this world's most beautiful cities, works in one of its loveliest buildings and lives in a monk's cell.

When he lunched with me he arrived on the back of a Vespa motor-scooter, having thumbed a lift from a youth who happened to be passing the Palazzo Vecchio as he came out from his office there.

We ate our lunch sitting at a table set up on a stone landing in a home for juvenile delinquents. They included boys who had been convicted of theft, and had then been given another chance and sent there instead of to jail, young vagrants and street-boys. In all there were some two score young Italians of 17–21 years of age. All of them had got on the wrong side of the law in one way or another. Yet there were no locks on the doors, no harsh regulations.

Looking after them was just one quiet-voiced smiling little old priest, Fr Secchiaroli of the Sons of Divine Providence. At any moment the members of his tough 'family' could have beaten him up and escaped. But it had never happened. Only one boy out of the 150 who had passed through the place since it was started had reverted to crime. Most saw it and loved it as a home, in many cases the first they had ever had. A number of the boys, despite their police records, are employed by the famous Florentine goldsmiths and jewellers. They spend their days working with gold and silver, having got their jobs on Fr Secchiaroli's recommendation. Not one has let him down.

"How does he do it?" I asked Mayor La Pira, as we ate our spaghetti together. "What is his secret?"

La Pira threw his arms wide open in a typical, exuberant gesture.

"Most members of his Order succeeded in time in acquiring, to some degree at least, one or other of Don Orione's many outstanding qualities. Fr Secchiaroli has something of Orione's force of personality, which came from a great love of people. That is his secret. Having got that he needs no bars, no harsh regulations, no police hovering in the background."

*

The big workers' centre in Turin was filled with engineering apprentices, many of them employed at the great Fiat works.

There were beds and good food for them, but there were also concerts, classes in art and musical appreciation, gramophone recitals and courses in everything from economics to philosophy.

"In addition," Fr Pollarolo, the Rector, told me, "we encourage them to learn to be good leaders in industry, ready to fight hard if necessary as shop stewards and trade unionists and to be able to give a constructive lead as well. Don Orione believed that the worker should fight for social justice and that everything possible should also be done by others to raise his dignity."

*

In his apartment in Rome I talked, as one ex-Communist to another, to Ignazio Silone, the famous novelist and Social Democrat Deputy whom Don Orione helped when he was a boy.

"Please, please," he said, "whatever you do, when you write about him, do not make Don Orione just a sort of Catholic Beveridge. To do so would be to diminish his size. Yes, he was concerned with charity as so many others have been, and with social justice, too. But his exceptional strength lay in the fact that in all he did he relied utterly and completely upon God."

Prologue

★

On April 7, 1949, Fr Paul Bidone, a priest of the Sons of Divine Providence, arrived in England. He could speak no English. In his hand he carried a ten-shilling note—his total fortune—and a slip of paper on which was the name and address of the one British contact known to his Congregation.

He brought with him also a firm belief that Divine Providence had a job for him.

On February 2, 1952, less than three years later, the first of many old men for whom he had started a home in South London took up residence there. The house had been bought at great cost, and with a heavy mortgage, but would have been far more expensive had it not been for the voluntary help which he received from local workers.

Another three years later, he opened a second house. The work among old men which he had started was meeting a local need. For it is the old who fare worst in the post-war Welfare State.

The generosity of the British people which had helped to make possible his extraordinary achievement was evidence that men were already beginning to recognise that social justice imposed from above, even though it be the will of the people, is not in itself enough. To it must be added Christian charity, in full measure and running over.

CHAPTER I

Son of the Sulli

When the Romans built the road through their camp at Pontecurone, they could hardly have been expected to know that they were creating a death-trap for motorists of the 20th century.

But the same road, straight as ever, still to this day runs through Pontecurone village. It is cobbled now, but down the middle of the rough cobbles run two lines of flat paving-stones set just about the width of a motor-car apart. So the motorists who rush from Milan to Genoa and from Genoa to Milan compete with each other for position. The weak ones go to the cobbles. The strong roar through the village dead in the centre of the road, following the paving-stones all the way.

In 1872, however, when Luigi Orione was born in Pontecurone, death had not taken control of the road; its traffic had changed very little for 2,000 years. Nor had the Communists taken control of the local council as they now have.

Even today, despite the main-road traffic, the 4,000 inhabitants, the three brick works and the textile mills employing 600 workers, it is just a sleepy, very dusty little Piedmontese town near the Lombardy border. In those days it must have been sleepier and dustier still.

In the lodge of the big house on the outskirts of Pontecurone lived Vittorio Orione, the *sulli* and his wife. As a *sulli* he was responsible for the maintenance of the local roads, getting the hard cobbles from the stream, fitting them together and laying them whenever repairs were required.

Among the simple country folk the bearded Vittorio, a former supporter of Garibaldi, was respected as a good craftsman, honest and solid. He was stern but just with the apprentices who worked in his gang. Sometimes he would lose his temper, shouting loudly at them with his powerful voice. But he never harboured anything against them and so he kept their respect.

He was so thrifty that to save money he would set off on Sunday night and walk as much as 40 miles when his work took him away from home. Unlike most of the men of the village he was never found in the wine shop, but was always seen at Mass on Sunday.

"With a good wife like that he couldn't go off the rails even if he had a mind to," an old man of 90 who still remembered him, told me.

"Not that there was anything of the hen-pecked husband about him. He was far too tough and strong for that." The villager's comment was no slur on Vittorio. It was a tribute to the immense character of his wife.

I spent a day talking to the old people of the village who remembered the Oriones from the days when Vittorio and Carolina were raising their family.

Most reliable and helpful of all to me in my enquiries was Signora Giovannina, a little old woman of 90, finishing her days in an old people's home run by the Little Missionary Sisters of Charity. She had a bright face, with alert laughing black eyes which responded to every point I made. There was no nonsense about her. She was 100 per cent down to earth. Her thin white hair was drawn tight over her head to a tiny bun at the back. Her memory took her back easily over the 80 years to the days when Luigi was a boy and she a somewhat older girl.

The family as a whole, she said, was a good one, but Luigi's mother, who came from the nearby village of Castel Nuovo, was very, very good indeed. She was a serious-faced, handsome woman and a holy woman, too—"an absolute saint". She believed in discipline, was strict but rarely handed out punishment. "One word from Mammie was enough." When she did punish, however, she did it thoroughly. She was "a good household manager, a good wife and a good parent".

Although she was herself an ordinary worker's wife she had exceptional authority among the other women of Pontecurone. The old lady recalled how Carolina would see other women gossiping or hear them swearing and would stop to correct them.

"But didn't they resent it, coming as it did from a woman who was just one of themselves?"

The old woman flung her hands in the air and opened her toothless mouth wide.

"Oh no. They esteemed her too well for that. They knew that she was good, no one could say a word against her and they admired her for what she was. It was the same when she urged them to go to Mass. They knew she not only went to Mass but always dropped into the church to pray when she was out. So they took it from her. She had a strong character, but she was good with it. No, no, there was no resentment."

Mention of Carolina's visits to the village church reminded my companion, Fr Paul Bidone, of a story he had heard about her.

"I heard that Luigi's mother offered some roses to Our Lady before he was born because she wanted special favours for him. Do you know anything about that?"

Again the little bony hands shot up into the air.

"Don't you believe it! She wasn't that sort. She was just as solid and practical in her devotions as in everything else. She wasn't the sort to do that."

The little peasant world of the Pontecurone of 80 years ago was re-created for me as she told of all the village women and children going each harvest-time to glean in the fields. The Orione family would be there in force: Luigi, the youngest boy; his brother, Alberto; and the wife of his oldest brother, Benedict.

As they moved across the fields gathering the fallen grain, the children would ease up and begin to play and Benedict's wife would stop to relax.

"Keep going, this is bread and bread is a sacred thing," Carolina would tell them. And again they took it without resentment, for she never spared herself.

To Carolina bread had an almost mystic significance, and the gathering of the grain took on the character of a sacramental. It was something so deep in her psychology and in her daily practice that it rooted itself deep in Luigi's mind; so much so that he carried it with him all his days, and a rule of each of the four religious Congregations he later established is that no bread shall ever be wasted.

Carolina's practice came to life again for me one day when I was travelling from Florence to

Rome with two prominent members of the Sons of Divine Providence. We had eaten one of the Italian railway's very adequate packed meals and each of us had a piece of bread-roll left. I was about to dispense with mine, along with the paper wrappings and cardboard plates and cups, when I noticed that my two companions were carefully wrapping theirs up in paper for later use.

*

Going from one villager to another I heard, over and over again, the story of the miraculously chiming bluebells. It is not easy to get the hard facts concerning the life of an Italian of peasant origin who has for long been acclaimed by the people as a saint and whose canonisation cause is already officially proceeding. The facts must be sorted out from a mass of legend; the ordinary, natural events from the supernatural; the everyday, from the exceptional and miraculous.

The devout Italian peasant accepts stories of miracles easily. Like his Spanish, Latin American, or Irish counterpart he has an unbroken link with the ages of the Faith, and as a result miracles are seen by him, not as something improbable but as what may be expected of those who work with God. To him miracles may seem to be the proof of sanctity. To one like myself, by nature sceptical and with such a very different background, they are little more than its by-products. The saint's spiritual life, his conquest of his own nature, his attitude to others, his works, these are the acid test. It is by these that his sanctity stands or falls.

Already, long before Luigi Orione's death, a great host of stories of miracles alleged and proved, had accumulated around his name. The easiest thing possible would be to write a book on the extraordinary and inexplicable occurrences in his life.

My line of approach was, therefore, to assume at the start that they were no more than so much folk-lore and to stick to that point of view unless the weight of evidence became such that they could not be thus dismissed.

Sig. Ernesto Sacchi lay sick when I interviewed him in his clean, cool bedroom. He was 83 years old, born in the same year as Luigi Orione. They had gone to school together. Sig. Sacchi at once began to tell me how when he was a very small boy Luigi went gathering a posy in the fields and as he picked a bluebell he was astonished to hear its bells tinkle like tiny chimes.

I interrupted him rather sharply.

"Look," I said. "That story may be true or it may be pure imagination. I can't prove it one way or the other all these years after it happened, and neither can you. But you can tell me something which is much more interesting to me. No flowers ever rang bells for me, nor for any of the people I ever knew. That sort of thing just puts Luigi Orione into a different category from the rest of us. It makes him someone whose life has no message for me. But he was an ordinary village boy. You played with him. You knew his moods, his temperament. That's what I want to know about."

At first when I began to spoil his best story for him Sig. Sacchi looked pained. But he was an intelligent man; like Vittorio Orione he had been the ganger in a team of *sulle*, a skilled worker in charge of others. He got my point, and I left his mind to work along different, more earthly lines for a few moments.

Then I turned suddenly to him again and shot a question which clearly startled him. "When he fought other boys at school and in the streets, did he fight clean or dirty?"

The old man thought hard. "He didn't fight often. He was a good boy and usually kept out of fights. But he had a terrible temper, and when he was roused he would fight fiercely for a moment and then it was all over. But it didn't happen often. I only saw it once or twice."

I pressed him further. "You say he fought in a temper and it was then quickly over. Did he box well? Did he punch the boys he was angry with in the face and knock them down, or did he butt them in the stomach, or what did he do?"

"He clawed at them, like this." The sick man's eyes momentarily blazed as, memory leaping back to the events of his boyhood days, he made a quick, fierce grab at the air with his fingers outstretched like claws. "He scratched and tore at them. He shouldn't have done it, it's no way to fight, and he was strong enough to beat them, anyway. But he was roused, you see. And he wasn't by nature very patient."

He said it almost guiltily, as though by his words he was betraying a friend, exposing something almost indecent which might destroy the reputation of someone whom he sought only to aid.

For me Luigi Orione grew perceptibly. He became real, and very human. His temper, his infrequent but dirty fights, these endeared him to me far more than his miraculously chiming flowers ever could.

I cross-checked Sig. Sacchi's story with 90-year-old Sig. Bozzi Federico whom I met in his parlour with his postman son and family. Sig. Federico, less inhibited because he had never had the same intimate friendship with Luigi, went further than Sig. Sacchi had done.

"He was a natural fighter," he said. "I don't mean by that that he was always fighting, although he could easily have been. Like his mother he was pious in a healthy way. But he was always ready to fight if he was provoked.

It was natural to him. You know what boys are. He knew very well that if he got into any fights he would not escape punishment from his mother who was too serious-minded to let that sort of thing pass. But he still fought from time to time because he was so quick-tempered. He didn't go around insulting other boys, but he found it difficult to take insults without flying into a rage."

*

In all, I found half a dozen old men and women who to a greater or lesser extent remembered Luigi as a boy. The picture which emerged from my questioning was of a boy with natural grace, good manners, quick intellect, and a temper. He was a good-looking lad with striking dark eyes, heavy eyebrows and rather overlarge ears and hands. The women were unanimous in remembering him as being attractive. "The sort, when he began to grow up, that girls took notice of, and would have liked to be seen with," one old woman told me so feelingly that I half suspected that years back she had felt that way herself. Then she added rather wistfully: "Those who knew him soon discovered that he had no thought for girls at all. From the time that he was a small boy he thought of himself as a future priest. So he had neither eyes nor thoughts for girls."

An old man confirmed this. "Even later on, the girls would have run after him, had he not been a priest," he told me.

As a small boy he had the normal amount of mischief in him and more than the usual amount of piety—without being 'pi' or falling under suspicion, among either the boys or the girls of his period, of being a 'sissy'. Equally, despite his occasional outbursts of fierce temper, he did not gain for himself a reputation either as a bully or as a young tough.

He was exceptional. That, too, emerged quite clearly. Each of the old men I talked to had taken it for granted that some day, in some way, he would make a name for himself. As I questioned them on this I became reasonably convinced that this was not just hindsight, not just being wise after the event.

At school he was the brightest in his form, learning a lot in a short time. In his formative years the dominant human influence over him was his mother. He was the brightest and most outstanding of her three sons. But there was no favouritism, and never any question of his being spoilt. As Signora Giovannina, my grand little 90-year-old witness put it: "She was proud of him. She was an affectionate mother to him but not demonstrative. There was none of this cuddling and kissing."

He returned her affection in much the same

way. To the end of her days he was immensely proud of her, made time to visit her and told her of all his successes and failures.

From her he learned by the time he was 13 to be as much at home in the church of the village to which the family had moved as in the cottage.

The church bell was rung, not by ropes, but by a boy who climbed right up into the little square belfry to do it. Luigi volunteered for the work but on the first day he rang the bell so hard and long that a man went to the priest next day to lodge a complaint. It seems not to have had much effect, however, for the villagers week after week continued to shout protests from the street, which Luigi pretended not to hear.

It is clear that, although he was recognised by the villagers as a more than usually well-behaved and respectful boy, he showed respect only where he thought it was due. The local priest, doctor and lawyer were sitting gossiping together on a seat in the mid-morning sun as the young Luigi went down the street. He took an incredulous look at them. How could they be sitting there at that time of the day when others were working in the fields and about their business? It conflicted with everything that his mother and his hard-working father had told him was right and proper. Indignantly he took a stick and stirred up in front of them a great cloud from the dust which lay thickly on the street. "Don't you know," he shouted, "that this is the time to work and not to sit idling in the sun?"

The matter was in due course reported to his mother who gave him one of her rare beatings. But, looking back on it years afterwards, he still thought that the shocked surprise he had seen on the faces of the three most solidly respectable citizens of the town was well worth the beating.

Making a real point by means of a demonstrative action was a practice he continued throughout his life although that was probably the first and certainly the last instance of it to earn him a beating from his mother.

In the church there was a huge crucifix with a very Italianate realistic Figure upon it. One Lent the young Luigi went out into the fields, found some Spinae Christi and plaited them into a formidable crown of thorns. He took it back to the church and placed it in position over the plaster crown which was already on the statue. The same crucifix, now in a glass case, is in the church to this day with Luigi's crown of thorns still, after 70 years, preserved.

This story is told to visitors by the pious natives of Pontecurone (the Communists, who dominate the town, have almost all come from distressed areas in other parts of North Italy). It is one which to them seems natural enough. To the Anglo-Saxon mind, four centuries away from the ages of the Faith, it seems somewhat macabre, suggesting almost sadistic tendencies in the young Orione. But then so do the robed skeletons of saints which lie in glass cases in some Italian churches, the skulls which repose on the desks of busy religious superiors, and the thousand and one other signs of an entirely different and, incidentally, healthier approach to the death of both God made Man and of man himself. What is quite certain is that in the whole life of Luigi Orione there is nothing to suggest anything but the very opposite of sadism.

Most of his spare time was spent around the little church, re-arranging the chairs after sodality meetings, preparing it for Sunday Mass and making himself generally useful.

It seemed natural enough, therefore, that at the age of 13, Luigi should be keen to begin his training as a priest. But how to do it when he had no money and knew of no one who would take him on?

One day when the snow was on the ground he set out walking to a deserted chapel outside the village of Fogliata. The chapel was falling to pieces but in it was a picture of the Madonna to which many of the country people had a great devotion. There, in front of the picture he prayed for guidance and then, with a gesture which later on was to become typical of him, he made a bargain with Our Lady. "Give me a place to try my vocation and I will rebuild this chapel for you," he promised her. Years later that is just what he did.

In due course he was given the opportunity to join the Franciscans and on September 4, 1885, he set out with his mother for the old Istituto San Antonio, a minor seminary for the training of Franciscans in the nearby town of Voghera. He took with him on a donkey cart all the things he would require—or at any rate all his parents could afford—packed in an old tin trunk.

He rang the friary bell, which for him signalled the entry to a life of which he had, though still such a boy, dreamed night and day for years.

The door was opened by an irritable, uncultured friar who took an amused look at the donkey cart and another at the battered trunk.

"Where do you come from?"

"From Pontecurone."

The friar burst out laughing.

"Pontecurone! Why, that is the place where everyone has goitres," he said offensively.

Then he looked again at the boy's luggage and kicked it contemptuously with his toe.

"And what do you call this?" he sneered.

At that moment the superior appeared in the door and rescued the hurt and indignant Luigi from his tormentor. He was a kindly man who quickly made the boy feel at home.

The ancient friary is today the property of the

Sons of Divine Providence, founded by that same Luigi Orione.

Even now, restored and to some extent modernised, it still has all the draughts and disadvantages of an old building. Seventy years ago, conditions there must have been indeed Spartan. There were less than ten postulants and just five friars, living in a building which could have housed many times that number. Even so funds were so short that they only kept going with difficulty.

Six months after his arrival, on Maundy Thursday, 1886, just three days before he was to be clothed with his Franciscan habit, Luigi fell seriously ill. A chill quickly turned to pneumonia. In the circumstances this was not surprising. The 14-year-old boy had been preparing himself for Easter Sunday, when the ceremony was to be held, by prayer and study, not only all day but all night too. To ensure that he should not spend his night in sleep, he put pieces of wood in his already hard and uncomfortable bed. Then, whilst the other boys slept, he would spend the night kneeling on the cold stone floor. He had done that throughout the chilly month of March.

On Maundy Thursday he fainted in the church. He was taken to the infirmary. It was found that he had pneumonia and his parents were sent for. Luigi, with a raging temperature, heard from his room in the enclosure his father and mother arrive in the adjoining parlour; and for one of the few times in his life he heard Carolina weeping. Boylike, he assumed that she had been told that he was dying, and so he prepared himself for death. "I was quite resigned to the thought of death," he said later. "It filled me with no distress at all, but it did distress me to hear my mother weeping so loudly."

For two weeks he was critically ill. One day whilst he still hung between life and death he dreamed that he was one of a long queue of postulants who were dressed, not in the Franciscan habit, but in one which he did not know. A few days later, when he had started to mend, the doctor advised his superiors that after such a severe attack of pneumonia he would not be strong enough to continue life at the friary and that he should therefore be told that he would not be able to become a friar.

As soon as he had reached the convalescent stage his father and mother were again sent for, this time to take him away.

He was dismissed. For just six months it had seemed that he would realise his one ambition, the thing which had dominated his thoughts throughout his childhood. Now it was at an end.

It was a very weak and disappointed young Luigi who jolted along in the donkey cart down the cobbled road from Voghera to Pontecurone.

CHAPTER II

Tempest in the Tower

CAROLINA was disappointed at the turn that events had taken. Vittorio clearly had mixed feelings about the matter.

Now Luigi would be able to keep himself in bread and butter and help with the family's meagre finances, too. Sooner or later he would find where his vocation lay. Meanwhile, as soon as he was strong enough, he could come and work with him. It would be a healthy open-air life, which was just what was needed if he was not to slip into tuberculosis.

Throughout the summer of 1886 Luigi worked in his father's gang. There were about a dozen men and boys from Pontecurone. When they went to work in Frugarolo, some distance away, they were joined by a team of similar strength composed of men from Lombardy. Vittorio was in charge of both.

Normally, there was competition between

teams. Now, because of the feeling which existed between the Lombards and the Piedmontese, the rivalry became somewhat intense. A meal of boiled corn and dried haddock was provided for them at midday and there were grumbles from the men from Lombardy that the Piedmontese were being given more than their share.

Vittorio devised a scheme whereby the men drew from two sets of straws, some short and some long. Those who drew the long ones got first choice. Soon, however, Luigi noticed that the Lombards were cheating, having come with their own long straws. After that Vittorio changed his method. He set the food in two rows and asked each one in turn whether he preferred left or right.

By the autumn Luigi was fit and strong again. Once more he was pressing his parents to be allowed to try his vocation for the priesthood. His mother required no persuading and at last in the autumn his father gave in.

This time, recalling the dream he had had during his delirium in the Franciscan friary at Voghera, it was to the recently formed Salesians of Don Bosco that he went. He arrived at their headquarters in Turin on October 4, 1886. There the great Don Bosco, whose work for street-boys and orphans had stirred all Italy, still presided over affairs.

At the Salesians' world headquarters in Turin,

I met 84-year-old Fr Giovanni Segalia who was with Luigi whilst he was a student at the Salesian seminary. He described him to me as "an exemplary student who was zealous in doing good". That sounded rather like a formal testimonial awarded to a student leaving college and so I asked him to illustrate the extent to which he was already at that time showing himself to be exceptional. His answer was convincing enough for anyone.

Before Luigi had completed his second year, and while he was still less than 16 years of age, he was chosen by his superiors to give lectures to his class-mates on religious matters and to preach sermons to them in their sodalities. This was quite unusual, reflecting both his own ability and the trust which the superior had in him. None of the others would have felt fitted for the task, but he could not only do it but be appreciated by his own contemporaries when he did it.

In addition to being admired for his intellectual and spiritual qualities he was liked for his jolly disposition and for the fact that he was good at games. He acted with the school's dramatic society and did it with enthusiasm and success.

The Salesians also found him attractive so that he made friends among both the boys of his own age and the members of the Community. In particular, he won the friendship of Don Bosco who took some of the classes himself.

This master-pupil friendship which was in fact friendship with one of the Church's greatest saints, meant an enormous amount to the sensitive, deeply spiritual boy. It was at Valdocco that he made his first Confession to Don Bosco and it was from him that he got a clear idea of where his own path of duty lay. The saint was both his superior and his Confessor.

The Salesians were taking boys off the streets and out of the appalling slums and were fitting them for life by teaching them trades. By means of this technical education they gave them a dignity which life had hitherto denied them. It was a work of great charity. But it was something much more practical and useful to them than mere doles and hand-outs.

Others who could not be accommodated or trained in this way were brought into clubs and so helped intellectually and spiritually. The work appealed to Luigi. His background of respectable poverty was close enough to the poverty that degrades for him to be able to feel for those whom the Salesians helped.

"Remember," Don Bosco told him, "we are always going to be friends," and Luigi warmed to the thought.

But in January 1888, when Luigi was doing his second-year course, Don Bosco was taken ill. With a typical gesture, when he heard that his friend and master was at death's door, Luigi offered his own life in exchange for that of the dying saint. But on the last day of January Don Bosco died.

Luigi's first reaction was to dedicate himself, more completely than ever before, to God and to His Church.

A story is told of which Fr Segalia says he had no knowledge at the time and which he read only long afterwards. It is as follows: When the saint's body was exposed for veneration Luigi took up his position as one of a 'guard of honour' composed of four of the most responsible of the boys. The faithful were coming from far and wide to venerate the saint whom so many had cause to love and Luigi knew that many of them longed to take home something which had been associated with him. So he cut some bread into small pieces, touched Don Bosco's body with them and then distributed them among the crowd. Whilst slicing the bread he cut one of his fingers deeply. To him there was no doubt whatsoever that Don Bosco was a saint and so he did what seemed to him to be the entirely natural thing in the circumstances: he touched the body with his wounded finger, which was at once healed.

Yet, despite his love for Don Bosco, and his friendship with the other Salesians at the school and his admiration for their good works, suddenly, at the end of his second year, just when he was at the point of joining their novitiate, he changed his plans and left for the diocesan seminary for secular clergy in Tortona.

Everyone, masters and boys alike, believed that he was peculiarly well qualified to become a Salesian. He was already teaching religion in a Salesian boys' club. There was general surprise, "but," Fr Segalia assured me, "we all knew that it must be all right, since what he was doing was approved by his superiors."

In fact, he had had from time to time, like most boys in his position, doubts about where his vocation lay. Could he best serve God with the Salesians or not? Months before, he had mentioned these doubts to Don Bosco himself who told him not to worry. "If you feel that it is the will of God that you should go elsewhere, you should go," he said. "Remember, we shall always be friends."

After the saint's death the doubts took more definite shape and form. One as conscientious as Luigi Orione knew that on such a matter there should be no doubts at all. For years he had been conscious that he had a mission to fulfil. Now he was convinced that, admirable though their work was, it was not with the Salesians. So, following what he felt to be the clear will of God, made crystal clear to him during the retreat which followed the conclusion of his second year of studies, he left and returned home.

*

It was not difficult for the Salesians, who had measured his spiritual calibre, to understand his action. It was much more difficult for the solid hard-working Vittorio to do the same. To him Luigi must have seemed unpredictable, if not positively wayward.

"If you can't make a success of your studies," he said, "you had better come back and work with me again until we see what is to happen to you."

Once more Luigi was a member of his father's gang of road repairers. But his heart was not in the work. With his mother's approval, he asked his parish priest to enquire into the possibilities of his being accepted at the seminary of his own diocese in the nearby cathedral city of Tortona.

For nearly a year he worked as a *sulli*. One day, in the autumn of 1889, he was working with the gang in Nizza Monferrato, 40 miles away from his home, when a letter was handed to his father. It was from the parish priest. Vittorio opened it quickly, read it and said, "Hurry up. We must go. You have been accepted at the seminary at Tortona."

Despite everything, he was obviously pleased, and hustled the boy off as quickly as he could. So, at 17 years of age, Luigi began his theological studies in Tortona's diocesan seminary for the training of secular priests.

To most people it would have seemed a much less romantic experience than life at a novice house which was still under the influence of the great Don Bosco. There must have been moments when Luigi himself wondered whether he had done wisely to leave the Salesians at Turin. For the seminary at Tortona was going through a bad patch. Discipline was weak, many of the boys were unruly. There was more than the usual, or permissible, amount of horseplay among them.

Everyone joked about Luigi's shabby clothes, his cheap shoes and the way in which he stinted himself to save every possible penny. They would throw bread under the table at meal times. Solemnly Luigi would pick it up and eat it. "Bread comes from God and must not be wasted," he would tell them, echoing his mother.

I have talked to old men who were boys there at the time and who have since grown wiser and more charitable with age. They now admit that it was not so much his poverty that made them want to rag him as the fact that he was so unlike the others. Ordinary youths get on most easily with those who are either no more than their equals or their inferiors in character. The young Orione was different, and in adolescent company that is a crime.

He was alert, intensely pious, far too preoccupied with his vocation to fit in at once easily with the others. He had certain gestures which seemed to them to be excessively dramatic—gestures of a type which are tolerated once a man has gained fame but which are resented, and mimicked, when he is still at the bottom of the ladder.

He had little desire to join in their games and none at all if it came to playing about when they should be working. Because he was so willing, they made him the seminary 'donkey' who did all the odd jobs and, in particular, fetched the water from the tap in the yard. Before long, Luigi had perfected a system which enabled him to carry four buckets at once. Gradually he settled in, partly by accustoming himself to their company, partly by influencing them in his own direction, partly by winning them over with his spirit of helpfulness.

Most of his spare time was given to aiding others. He helped to make their beds, to sweep their rooms. He tended them when they were sick. He might be poor, he might be unusual, but no group of boys could withstand such Christian charity in practice.

One who was permanently influenced by Luigi at this time was an unruly young seminarian who is now the Jesuit Fr Alberto Vaccari, of the Biblical Institute at the Vatican, and world famous as a Biblical scholar. Alberto had arrived at the seminary a year earlier than Luigi and had been carried along by the prevailing mood. He had become so unruly that his sense of vocation had almost disappeared, and his father had been told that he might have to take him away.

"1890–91 was the decisive year of my life," he told me, as we sat in his room in the Institute recalling his youth. "But for Don Orione I would probably not be in this cassock now. I owe my vocation to him."

"What was it about Luigi," I asked the old Jesuit, "that particularly influenced you?"

"Firstly, there was his example. He brought with him a mood and approach to his life and studies which we had either lost or never had. Secondly, his apostolic zeal, which he communicated to others. He was still in his teens and not yet a theological student; yet already he was planning his future work, which he saw quite clearly, and was seeking others who would co-operate with him in that work. Such a one was bound to be a powerful influence among the boys, for they were all essentially good."

Alberto became Luigi's closest friend in the seminary; that alone reflects how great a change must have been achieved in him. Luigi, from being an object of ridicule, was admired and respected by all the boys.

*

Across the road from the seminary, which is still a barrack-like building although considerably more comfortable today than it was then, is the 16th-century cathedral. Its architecture is commonplace. Its interior is somewhat gloomy. It is heavy with baroque decoration, dark wooden panels, big pictures and Italianate statues. There is little in its style or atmosphere to evoke devotion, at least in a visitor from the Northern end of Europe or from North America.

High up in the tower, above the sacristy, are some dusty living quarters, reached by a winding stairway, in which a lay custodian still resides. He sleeps in a large, bare room in one wall of which is a peep-hole looking straight down through the church to the altar.

When Luigi went to the seminary his parents were unable to pay the modest fees expected of them. So the Rector appointed him to help the cathedral sacristan. Along with another boy in similar circumstances he was sent to live in the room in the tower and there to act as custodian. On one occasion, as he kept guard at his peep-hole, he saw a man approaching the altar, clearly intent upon stealing the sacred vessels. Luigi gave the alarm and the would-be thief was sent packing.

As assistant sacristan he served Mass (sometimes as often as three times a day), was present at the recitation of the Rosary and helped to keep the place clean and tidy.

By this means he earned his bed and board. But it meant that when he was not in class much of his time was spent in and around the cathedral. As a consequence, most of his seminary life was lived apart from his colleagues. Always an individualist, he was able to follow his own highly individualistic course.

The Rector of the seminary grew increasingly fond of him. This again gave him opportunities to follow his own bent, while at the same time observing the rule of the highly-regulated seminary life, with its periods of silence, study and worship.

His studies, despite all his other duties, went well, although much of his reading of dogmatic and moral theology, canon law and scripture must have been done at night and in odd moments. The marks awarded him, as his reports of the period reveal, were always high. To those who teased him because he took his studies so seriously, he replied: "Of what use to the Church is an ignorant priest?"

At recreation, he joined in the games as lightheartedly as anyone else. He had long ago learned from Don Bosco that this was a qualification required of anyone who was going to work among boys. No one ever quite knew what he was going to do next.

But once when an entertainment had been arranged for one of the professors he was asked if he would care to make a speech. He agreed, and everyone supposed that it would be something brief and suitably trivial. Instead, he delivered himself of a brilliant speech, acclaimed as a wonderful piece of rhetoric, which left his hearers dumbfounded. He sat down to a great round of applause. From that day, to the regard which he had earned for his charity was added also respect for his intellect and ability.

His piety was impressive although he was careful not to make it obtrusive. Those who associated most closely with him soon learned how much of his thought was focused upon his four great loves: The Cross, the Holy Eucharist, Our Lady and the Pope. His face took on a new expression and his voice a new tone when he spoke of them.

*

For long he had been wondering whether he could do some sort of work like that done by Don Bosco in Turin, possibly by starting a boys' club.

One day an orphan boy who was in trouble came to him. Along with some other boys he had been playing truant from school and the teachers, because he was an orphan, had threatened to throw him out.

From him Luigi learned of the bad company which a number of the poorer boys of Tortona were keeping. Many of them were playing truant, some had deserted their schools altogether. Day after day they would go to the local barracks and there associate with soldiers much older than themselves both in years and in experience of the seamier side of life. The soldiers gave them food but they threatened to corrupt them as well.

Luigi called them together in a little old, disused church from which the Blessed Sacrament had long since been removed. What they needed was healthy fun and recreation, instead of the sort of entertainment they were getting at the barracks.

He brought into service what he had learned of amateur theatricals in Turin, mimicking tragedians, doing conjuring tricks and, of course, talking to the boys. He made them sing hymns, leading them with his own strong if not particularly tuneful voice and took them for organised walks in the country. And, of course, he taught them their catechism.

Before long they constituted themselves a highly unconstitutional club. In order to keep them together, he sought and obtained permission for them to come freely to his room in the cathedral tower.

From that day on, his life and the events surrounding it took on a quality which can only be called fantastic. Anything could happen. In fact anything did happen and, to this day, does still happen to those upon whom his mantle has fallen.

When the first orphan boy came to him, Luigi had said: "You'll see what fruitful seed you and I are going to sow." Those were prophetic words.

Night after night the boys came to his room. They came in scores. Soon they came in hundreds. Always there were little urchins tramping up the stairs asking for Luigi Orione. They were not little plaster saints. Had they been that, he would not have been working amongst them. The noise they made could be heard all around the cathedral and, quite literally, above it, too, as they congregated in his dusty room high up in the tower.

Some of the Canons of the cathedral were beginning to question whether the Rector's decision to allow this 20-year-old youth to have his boys in his room had been such a good idea after all. To discourage him they reduced his meagre salary. But the club and the noise continued.

Then one day he went to the Bishop, Mgr Igino Bandi, to ask whether he and his boys might have the use of the private garden attached to the Bishop's residence.

Perhaps it was that the Bishop had heard the complaints about the noise which now disturbed the calm of the cathedral; maybe it was just that he liked the unpredictable youngster's cheek; or it may have been that Luigi's reputation stood so high that the Bishop was prepared to grant him exceptional favours. But whatever the reason, on July 3, 1892, he granted his request.

The boys, and the noise, were thus transferred, most nights, across the road. Calm was restored in the cathedral and the Canons could be left to enjoy it. But the calm of the secluded episcopal garden quickly disappeared.

An immediate consequence was that the Bishop was soon having to listen to long and vigorous protests from his own mother who lived with him. The garden, she said, was being destroyed. What had been an episcopal garden was now a bear-garden. The Bishop, however, approved of what Luigi was trying to do and withstood the domestic storm.

The important thing, from young Orione's point of view, was that the Bishop, having thus been brought into the picture, had given his blessing to the project which was now duly regularised and recognised as a boys' club. The club was put under the protection of St Louis and named "The Club of St Louis". It was given a sympathetic, wise and kindly Canon, Mgr Novelli, as a chaplain and president. Another student, older than Luigi, was appointed to work with him.

Things moved quickly. Joseph Perosi, the cathedral's choirmaster, agreed to train a choir from among the boys, and his son Lorenzo Perosi (later to become Mgr Perosi, famous composer and master of the Sistine Chapel Choir) composed a hymn for the street-boys' choir in honour of their patron saint.

The club clearly met a real need and was absolutely in accord with the new spirit released by the work of Don Bosco.

It was a period of acute economic depression. Extreme poverty was widespread. Large numbers of boys lived for most or all of their time on the streets. Orphans fended for themselves as best they could. Moreover it was also, in Italy, a period of sharp anti-clericalism, to which the new Marxist ideas, which were widespread, had given a political and often an atheistic edge. The masses of the working class were visibly slipping away from the Church into a mood of indifference at the best and, at the worst, of organised hostility.

About any political consequences of his activities Luigi probably knew little and cared less. What mattered was that right there in ancient Tortona, within the shadow of the cathedral and within easy reach of the seminary, there were boys with bodies and souls both of which were left hungry.

It was his job, as he saw it, to satisfy that hunger and above all to stop the moral rot which accompanied years on the streets.

★

The new club needed premises. It had long since outgrown the room in the tower. Something more was needed than a somewhat amorphous club which brought them together at nights in no more than a semi-organised way. The movement required a stable core. The obvious answer, to Luigi Orione's mind, was a boarding school for all types of boys, which might be a centre from which he could produce men who would help to bring their generation back to God, and could also be the means of fostering vocations for the priesthood—for Italy was desperately short of priests.

He went to the Bishop, told him his views and put his scheme before him. The Bishop having conceded so much, this new step which was asked of him was logical enough.

"How can I help?" the Bishop asked.

"By giving me your approval and blessing."

"Very well, you have both."

With some courage, and also probably with

some trepidation, the Bishop told him that if he could find suitable premises he could go right ahead.

Like the granting of the use of his garden, this was a step which had considerable consequences.

Perhaps the Bishop thought at the time that the idea that a 20-year-old seminarian should start a ragged school was too wild, too ambitious ever to reach fruition. Perhaps he sensed instinctively that this was no ordinary seminarian, asking no ordinary favour, and that the consequences would be far from ordinary too.

At any rate, Luigi went off with a song in his heart, but not a penny piece in his pocket, to find a suitable place. He was ready to scour the town from end to end. In particular he would search the streets of San Bernardino, the poorest end of the town and the one which had drifted furthest from the Church and where accordingly anti-clericalism was most rife.

He set out from the Bishop's residence at once. The fact that he had no money and was still a minor did not worry him in the least. He had Divine Providence on his side. Hardly had he started his search when he met Louis Stassano, the brother of a boy in his own club. Louis asked where Luigi was going.

"I'm off to start a school for boys and I've got permission from the Bishop."

"Where is it? I would like to go to it myself."

"I'm just trying to find a suitable place."

"My father has an empty house which would just suit your purpose."

Louis' father was an active Catholic, a member of the Society of St Vincent de Paul, and so himself interested in good works. In Tortona at that moment he had a property of which he wanted to dispose. It was right in the heart of San Bernardino, a three-storied building left to him by his brother. Louis told Luigi all about it, and then and there Luigi decided to go and see if he could persuade the boy's father to let him have it.

The project was explained to Signor Stassano who agreed that a school was necessary and desirable. But he had misgivings about the extreme youth of its promoter. And there was, of course, the small matter of payment.

"How much do you want?" asked Luigi.

"Four hundred lire (£16) a year, with the first year's rent paid in advance. But you are only a boy. Have you got it?"

"No. But don't worry about that; I'll soon have it with the help of Divine Providence."

Stassano told him that if he could raise the money within the week he could have the property. If not, he might consider the matter closed.

"With the help of Divine Providence anything can be done," Luigi said.

But none the less, as the older man shut the

door on the enthusiastic young seminarian, he probably thought that that was the end of that particular story.

Luigi set off back to his room to think—and pray—things over. On the way he met a woman named Angelina Poggi.

"Hello, Luigi, what are you doing around here?" she called to him as he passed.

"I'm going to open a boys' school and I've got the permission of the Bishop."

"I've got a nephew who needs some schooling. What are your fees? What would I have to pay if I sent him to you?"

"Just whatever you can afford."

Angelina thought for a moment.

"If I give you 400 lire, for how long will you keep him?"

"I'll keep him to the end of his studies."

At that moment Luigi was prepared to promise to keep the boy to the end of his life if need be.

Angelina thought again.

"All right. I'll give you the fee at once and he can be your first pupil."

Luigi dashed back to Stassano's house as quickly as he could, put the 400 lire down in front of the astonished follower of St Vincent de Paul and got down to talking business at once.

When he left the house he carried in his pocket a receipt for one year's rent and the agreement.

His project had been put before the Bishop, had received his approval and had been made a reality all in the course of a single morning. Now he would get the school filled and started at once. He would now report progress to the Bishop.

But whilst he had been away, representations had been made to the Bishop by people who were anxious about the project. What, they asked, would Luigi do next? They urged prudence upon the Bishop. So Mgr Bandi had second thoughts—and who should blame him?

Luigi, blissfully unconscious of what had been happening, met the senior sacristan when he got back.

"The Bishop has been asking for you. We've been looking for you everywhere," he said. "He has sent for you three or four times."

"I want to see him, too," said the excited Luigi.

He went straight in to see the Bishop. One look at Mgr Bandi's face was enough to tell him that all was not well.

"A few hours ago I gave you my blessing on your plan for a school. I must now withdraw it. The whole idea must be dropped."

"But I'm sorry, my Lord, it can't just be dropped like that," said Luigi, humbly but earnestly.

The Bishop banged the table but Luigi went on with his story.

"I've found the premises, and I've paid the

first year's rent. We've simply got to see it through."

The Bishop asked for the details. When he heard them, he was left in no doubt that this was Divine Providence at work.

"Kneel down," he said, "I'll give you my blessing again, and I'll never take it away."

Luigi Orione shortly afterwards announced that his new school, the first boarding school in the town, would be opening on October 16.

CHAPTER III

Founder Aged Twenty

Luigi, at the age of 20, was both a student and the founder of a boarding school. Even more surprising, while still a seminarian he had become the founder of an order. The Bishop appointed him rector of the school, and an older student was detailed to give a hand as well. Luigi, whose project it was, had the principal responsibility for the scheme and was to teach in the school of which he was the head.

Before the opening date there was a lot of work to be done, and Luigi's studies had still to go on as usual. So, too, had his work as assistant sacristan at the cathedral, upon which he depended for paying his own fees.

The new premises were in a filthy state and full of rubbish. Curiously enough, the last tenants had been the local branch of the Marxist Socialist party, and their slogans were still all over the walls. One room, which was to be the main school room, had been used for their dances.

Among the boys who presented themselves on the opening day were the nephew of Angelina Poggi and the two Stassano boys.

I visited one of the Stassanos, Dominico, in his home in Tortona and from him got a picture of what the first days were like. To say that they were hard is an understatement. The surprising thing to anyone today is that parents sent their boys there at all.

The entirely different conditions and circumstances of the period must, however, be borne in mind. There were practically no schools for working-class and lower middle-class boys at all. Because of the shortage of priests it was often extremely difficult for practising Catholics to get even normal instruction in the catechism for their children. And, of course, life for such people was hard in any case. They had little experience of comfort and none of luxury. And there was always Luigi Orione popping in and out to make life tolerable for the boys he loved.

"We all nearly starved in the school, but we were happy none the less," Dominico told me.

He illustrated his point by recalling how his father, happy about his boys' spiritual welfare but not so certain about their physical well-being, crept one night into what after all was his own property. He found them shivering in a bed with insufficient blankets. They were hungry into the bargain. He disappeared and in due course crept in again, bringing with him some bread. "You'll starve," he whispered, "if you don't eat this. Share it with the others or they may die too."

Night after night he did the same thing and always the same whispered conversation took place in the darkness of the dormitory, whilst Luigi slept on the bare boards at the other end.

"How are you tonight?"

"I'm hungry."

Then would come the bulky parcel of bread. When it had been safely slipped under the bedclothes, he would creep away again and the bread would be passed around.

Luigi would go the round of the beds night after night. If a boy was restless or had a bad dream, he would get up from his position on the floor and come quietly to the side of his bed.

"I'm sorry you aren't sleeping well," he would say. "Pray to your guardian angel for sleep and you'll be all right."

Then he would lie down on the floor beside the bed until the boy dozed off again.

"What," I asked Dominico Stassano, "was discipline like? Were punishments severe and frequent?"

"Usually it was enough for the boys to see Orione's flaming eyes for them to avoid committing the same offence twice," he replied.

Over and over again, incidentally, as I travelled Italy, following in the steps of Don Orione, I heard references to his eyes. Their first effect was usually profoundly disturbing; they were so penetrating, so unusual. I have heard them called "luminous—like a cat's". I have heard them called "the kindest on earth". A small boy in Milan once described them as "just like a pair of headlights on a car. You couldn't miss them and you felt yourself drawn towards them." Those who had seen them blaze with indignation or anger had had an experience they would never forget.

Any boy who incurred Luigi's just wrath would find himself confronted by a pair of blazing eyes.

"You have sin on your conscience and that is damnable," he would tell them. Then the anger would turn to pity and he would try to put the offender back on the rails again.

"No one was expelled that year," said Dominico. He counted on his fingers. . . . "And there were six vocations for the priesthood."

The school altogether housed some 130–135 boys with more than another 100 coming as day-boys. By the second year their numbers had doubled, so that the house was too small. Larger premises were needed. This time he leased the old convent and church of Santa Chiara.

The original house went out of Luigi's hands

but he always had an affection for it. Years later he was able to buy it and it was made the mother-house of his first order of nuns who still use it as such.

Long before they moved out of the old premises Sig Stassano had passed back Luigi's 400 lire to him to help him with his work. Luigi tried to pay him a second time, taking with him a small handful of notes.

"Where did they come from?" asked Stassano.

"From benefactors who want to help on my work."

"Then use them for that. Don't give them to me."

Stassano was a small landowner and worked with a few farm hands on his own land. He could afford to lose his 400 lire, but not without some sacrifice.

The new and larger school required more teachers, and Luigi managed to persuade lay teachers employed at the State school to come and work part-time there, giving their services.

★

In the second year there was a case of indiscipline which Dominico vividly remembered.

A professional man in a nearby village had two sons at the school. One day one of them committed a grave and scandalous sin in the local church. The matter came to the ears of Luigi. The nature of the sin would in itself have infuriated him, but the fact that it had been committed inside the church made the old temper of his childhood days flare up.

He beat the boy so hard and so many times that his nose bled and he was ill for several days. The beating took place in front of all the boys among whom was the culprit's own brother. Seeing his brother being beaten in such a way he ran out and fought Luigi, trying to stop him.

News of the affair reached the boys' father who threatened to take Luigi to court. But after a brief conversation between them the father went away, leaving his two sons still in Luigi's care. Even more striking, one of the two later became a priest in Don Orione's own Congregation. Dominico was able to tell me that the episode in no way made the boys who had witnessed it love Luigi less. Never at any time did they fear him, and the boy himself, recognising in Don Orione's anger a deeply felt and just indignation, bore him no resentment.

★

Two episodes from this period illustrate his characteristic refusal to let anyone or anything deter him from following his chosen course and what he was convinced was that of Divine Providence.

The first was told me by Bozzi Federico, the 90-year-old man in Pontecurone.

News of Luigi's school soon reached his home village and naturally caused some excitement there. Relatives of the Oriones who had not in the past shown any particular interest in his fate, were suddenly proud to claim him as their own.

A maiden aunt sent him some money, which he spent on the boys. In due course she swept into the school, asking to be told how he had used it. "But she left with a flea in her ear," Sig. Federico told me, "and with Luigi telling her, 'There are no *eccezionali personali* (privileged persons) here.'"

I am indebted to Sig. Federico and the late Mgr Lorenzo Perosi, Master of Music at the Sistine Chapel, for this second story which concerns them both.

At the age of 20, Luigi, Lorenzo and Bozzi got their call-up papers together. Seminarians were not exempt from military service. But Luigi, although more patriotic than many, had no desire to drop all his work and disappear into the forces to the detriment of his projects and studies.

He had been working hard, was very thin, and clearly not very strong. He decided to do everything possible to get himself rejected on medical grounds.

He turned up for his medical examination in his brother's clothes, partly because he did not want to go dressed as a seminarian (the anti-clericals liked nothing better than to direct a young man studying for the priesthood into the army) and partly because, being too big for him, the clothes accentuated his thinness.

They waited together in a big hall. Luigi walked up and down it almost fiercely and at great speed. Bozzi tried to keep up with him for a while but was soon exhausted.

"When are you going to stop? I'm getting tired," he said.

"I'm going on for as long as I can and as hard as I can," was the reply. "I want to exhaust myself and to make my heart beat as fast as possible. I want them to find me unsuitable."

When they went to undress together, Bozzi noticed a wide rubber band around Luigi's body, going across his chest and under his armpits.

"Why have you got that on?" he asked.

"For the same reason. I've soaked it in vinegar because there is a theory that it temporarily creates a condition which a doctor may mistake for tuberculosis. It may help, you never know."

To Lorenzo Perosi he confided that for three months he had eaten nothing fattening and had existed for the most part on salads. Lorenzo was rejected because he lacked several inches on his chest measurement.

Whether these devices in fact had anything to do with it or not, Luigi, too, was rejected and returned to his work in Tortona rejoicing.

*

What did his fellow seminarians think of their unusual colleague? They had long ago, right from the start, decided that he was odd. Then they had come round to the idea that he was admirable—but still odd. Now, with his successful college, they thought that he was both odder and more admirable than even they could have imagined.

He was constantly apt to astonish them with the unpredictable things he did. There was, for example, the occasion when a number of them were celebrating the feast of St Aloysius Gonzaga. A large gathering had assembled in a village in another part of the diocese. A group of the seminarians, Luigi among them, had gone over to support it.

Luigi quietly disappeared from the group, and the next thing they knew was that he had appeared on the platform and was delivering an impassioned, but entirely unauthorised, speech to an appreciative crowd. While still a deacon, he had been given the exceptional privilege of being allowed to preach, so that it was no new experience to him to hold an audience.

"What did you all think of that sort of thing?" I asked an old priest who had been one of their number. "Did you resent it as exhibitionism? Did you, among yourselves, suspect him of pride or arrogance?"

"No," he replied, "we had long ago learned that he was not guilty of these things. We all had the idea that he was unusual. Some started by thinking him odd. But all came in time to esteem him especially for both his ability and his transparent sincerity. None of us thought of him as not being genuine."

Fr Alberto Vaccari, S.J., of the Biblical Institute, agreed when I discussed it with him in the Vatican. "His tumultuous energy might easily have led him astray, but he controlled himself and by the grace of God and with the help of good friends he learned to use it in the right way. It must be admitted that, but for the grace of God, with his vitality and naturally rebellious spirit he might have become a demagogue, a rebel or an enormous influence for evil instead of good. The same abilities and qualities used in the wrong way might have had appalling results. He was at that time, and remained throughout his life, a veritable dynamo; full of new ideas, like a force which could never stand still."

*

Founder Aged Twenty

On Holy Saturday, April 13, 1895, Luigi was ordained in Tortona Cathedral by Mgr Bandi, and became the Don Orione whose name before long was a legend throughout Italy. Despite all his many interests and activities, he had prepared himself well, both intellectually and spiritually, for what he regarded as the greatest event of his life.

On Easter Sunday he celebrated his first Mass, in the church of Santa Chiara, attached to the disused convent which he had converted into a school. Boys from the school served his Mass and filled the church. They were dressed, by special permission of the Bishop, in what in practice became the habit of the embryo Congregation of which he was the founder.

Among the first members of his Religious Institute was Don Charles Sterpi. A fruitful personal friendship and working alliance grew up between the two young men which endured over the years. Don Sterpi in a very special way supplemented Don Orione, restraining him when he was at his most impetuous, consolidating the things he initiated, following through the ideas which came bubbling out of him like a torrent. The two men worked together perfectly, precisely because in so many ways they were opposites. Their lives fitted together like a metal worker's die and counter-die.

This aspect of their relationship was brought

home to me in particular and at a very ordinary human level by Mgr Lorenzo Perosi. At table, he said, they normally sat side by side. Don Orione would lead the conversation, vigorously, almost aggressively, with a wealth of gestures, as he ate. Don Sterpi would listen silently, nodding his approval, at times maybe quietly expressing dissent. The meal over, Don Orione would take his table napkin, screw it up in a heap, throw it on to the table and dash off to his next job. Don Sterpi would take up the crumpled napkin again, straighten it out, fold it meticulously and put it into its ring. Then he would unobtrusively leave the room and proceed to carry into action the ideas which his colleague had thrown to the four winds.

★

Don Sterpi had come from slightly higher up the social scale than Don Orione. His parents owned their own home and vineyard, and his father was Mayor of the small village in which they lived.

Although he was three years the younger of the two, Charles Sterpi was already in the seminary at Tortona when Luigi Orione arrived. Charles was a promising student and was sent from the major seminary whilst he was studying theology to supervise the juniors.

One day, when Luigi with a group of his boys was coming away from a shrine above the seminary he met Charles. Luigi was 23 and near his ordination. Charles was 20. They already knew each other and so Luigi told him of his work. He asked if he would care to help in it, if the Bishop consented. Charles said that he would. It was not long before Luigi had got the Bishop's permission, but in peculiar circumstances.

At Luigi's school was a particularly unruly boy, a member of a very prominent Catholic family in Tortona whose father had recently done the Bishop a favour.

Luigi decided that the boy was a disruptive influence and created too much work and anxiety for the few helpers, and so should be dismissed. His father, however, went to the Bishop and asked him to intervene.

The Bishop did so. "Why," he asked Luigi, "do you want to expel this boy? He is not a wicked boy. He may be unruly, but he is not bad."

"I have no desire to send any boy away," Luigi replied. "But I have no helpers. I would gladly take him back if I had some student to help me."

The Bishop agreed that a helper should be provided and submitted a list of the names of his best theological students.

Luigi pointed to the name of Sterpi.

"I'll have him."

"But he is the best student of them all. How can I spare him?"

"He is the only one of those whom you have offered me who could deal with the boys."

Luigi Orione, as usual, got his man. As usual, too, he had chosen the right one.

In his own way Don Sterpi was as strong as Don Orione himself. But where the one was like an uncontrollable storm with his words, the other was silent. Yet from the start Don Sterpi showed that he had enough strength of character to be able to control boys with a single look, just as Don Orione did.

But while Don Orione remained a volcano to the end Don Sterpi consciously and deliberately remodelled himself in such a way as to supplement the other. He became sweet and mild. Where Don Orione trod vigorously and heavily, Don Sterpi walked as lightly as a fly.

He was a man of great common sense and his was always the common-sense view. Don Orione's was in its intuitive way something higher. Yet he also needed the other man's down-to-earth realism.

Over the years, as the partnership developed, each knew his own role. Each kept his place. Each completed the other.

★

Luigi's turbulent energy was such that before long his newly acquired Santa Chiara convent, like his first house, had become too small to house all his boys and to be the centre of all his many activities. So, while still retaining the second house, he opened a third at Mornico Losanna, to which he sent as director Don Paul Albera who later became Bishop of Mileto. This latest school provided agricultural education for boys from peasant families, so putting into effect a very practical idea which he had for some time entertained.

The Bishop had asked Don Orione to continue as full-time rector of his school, but in practice his time was spread over a host of activities. Everything he did revealed the urgent need for something more. Every project tended to lead to a scheme for another one.

As a teacher Don Orione was a tremendous success. He conveyed easily to the boys the knowledge he wished to impart. In particular, he awoke in them a great interest in their national literary heritage, making them enthusiastic readers of his own favourite authors, Manzoni, Pellico, De Amicis and, above all, Dante.

For Dante he had a love which undoubtedly influenced profoundly much of his thinking. He steeped himself in Dante's thought and could recite from memory long passages from *The Divine Comedy*. In later life he would with the same certainty as Dante himself jokingly assign the exact position in hell which he thought some well known person—sometimes even a Bishop or a Cardinal—might be expected to occupy at some later date.

Around him now worked a group of priests and lay teachers. All lived in conditions of great privation, but together they formed a happy, purposeful team, with absolute trust in the ability of their captain, under God's guidance, to lead them on.

It was not surprising that they had their opponents. They were all young and Don Orione himself was still a very newly ordained priest. To older men with a vested interest in things being left undisturbed he seemed no more than a headstrong upstart who sooner or later would take a fall. And there was a certain amount of jealousy, too.

These people were often in high places in the Church, and they passed on their doubts and suspicions to the Bishop. In time Mgr Bandi began once again to grow uneasy about the rapid tempo of the little group's advance. Had he acted wisely or not in allowing this thing to be launched in his diocese and in giving this wild, strong-willed, unpredictable young man his head?

Maybe some day a crash would come and he would live to regret his part in it. One can understand his anxiety and sympathise with it.

So, not long after Luigi's ordination, there came a period of strained relations between the Bishop and the young priest. Some of the Bishop's advisers were pressing heavily for Don Orione to be switched to ordinary parish work. To make him a curate would bring him down a peg or two. They suggested that his place should be taken by another, older man, Don Albera.

"It is all right helping Orione," they said, "but his movement may grow and cause trouble."

Don Orione, careful not to cut himself off from diocesan life and genuinely anxious to work humbly with his Bishop, was out preaching somewhere every Sunday. But that was not enough. The Bishop finally yielded to pressure and said that Don Albera would be appointed superior at the school.

Don Orione and the devoted little band of priests around him were already talking of the foundation of a new Congregation and were planning its development. If the Bishop's proposal were to be enforced it would mean the end of all that.

So Don Sterpi and another priest, Don Goggi, went to the Bishop and made representations on behalf of them all.

"We gave our pledge to Don Orione," they

said, "that all our lives and activities would be joined to his. We cannot and will not do the same for anyone else. We shall have to withdraw from the school. We are, therefore, at your disposal for appointment in the diocese."

The Bishop saw that if they withdrew the new work would crash at once. At the same time he did not want to give in.

"You mean that if I do this I shall destroy this work?" he asked them. "I will never do that."

But he gave them no new assurance and they left dissatisfied with the Bishop still angry and the matter unresolved.

Then Don Orione himself went to see the Bishop. An 80-year-old priest who was his spiritual director at the time told me that those who knew his fiery temperament wondered at the wisdom of the move. If the Bishop was still angry and determined and Don Orione dug in his heels neither would get anywhere. If Don Orione lost his temper anything might happen.

They need not have worried. For the first time Luigi Orione revealed to his collaborators that he had not only fire, drive, vigour and confidence. He had patience and tact, too, when required. He was a diplomat. And as the years passed this side of his character became perhaps just as well known and as impressive as the other.

"The biggest job he had at that time, and for

that matter throughout his life," the same old priest told me, "was self-control. It was not easy for him to curb that impetuous nature. He never suffered from overweening pride although some of his actions might have suggested this to those who did not know him. What they could never know about was the battle he fought all day long with himself."

Don Orione's character was revealed, he said, by his reaction whenever he received a letter expressing disagreement with his own views or asking for something to which he could not easily accede. First he would seize some paper and start writing with enormous vigour in his huge, untidy scrawl, quickly filling great pages with only a few sentences on each. Then there would be a great deal of crossing out, with the pen working less noisily and fiercely. Finally he would tear up the letter and start again, this time quietly giving in. In other words, his first reactions to anything which did not strike an immediate chord were volcanic. Then he got control of them and kept control from there on. If he showed toughness in organising others it was nothing compared to that which he used against himself.

*

The 'little work' was all the time becoming bigger. Don Orione, a man of action who was also a man of prayer, recognised the dangers that might lurk in this rapid growth. It would be so easy for them in these heady first days to be carried along by a great rush of activity which might in time become an end in itself. What was needed was a power-house of prayer to support them in all they did. He found the answer in the "Hermits of Divine Providence"—a group of men who, as the name implies, would live hermits' lives, spending their days in prayer and simple, prayerful work.

He submitted his plan to Pope Leo XIII, who took it up at once and wrote approvingly of it. The first of Don Orione's Congregations to be canonically formed was that of the Hermits, the first of whom was clothed in the religious habit on September 8, 1898, little more than three years after its founder's ordination.

The Little Work of Divine Providence, now a world-wide religious Congregation, had in effect begun in 1892 when, on July 3 of that year whilst Luigi was still a seminarian, the Bishop inaugurated the episcopal Oratory of St Louis—at that time a boys' club meeting in the cathedral tower. The *Decretum Laudis* quotes this date as that of the initiation of the Congregation.

The Hermits established themselves in the old monastery of St Albert of Butrio, near Pavia, in the Apennine Mountains. According to an ancient legend Edward II of England, whom history records as having been murdered in Berkeley Castle, escaped to Italy and ended his days in prayer and penance in this monastery high up in the mountain. The Hermits later moved to another monastery on Mount Soracte, also in the Apennines, but near Rome. They began as a handful of men, mainly of peasant origin, whose lives, prayer and work were all made as simple as possible. Don Orione did not intend to found an order of great contemplatives. He saw the Congregation as a purely practical, natural and necessary adjunct to his other work.

CHAPTER IV

Flying Sparks

LENIN, in 1901, founded his paper *Iskra*, the *Spark*. When he did so he wrote, "a newspaper is not only a collective propagandist and collective agitator, but also a collective organiser." And in his article "Where to Begin?" he declared that the paper would be "the main thread by following which we would be able to develop, deepen and expand. . . ." Around it the infant Bolshevik party did indeed expand, so that in time the *Spark* was seen—and felt—all over Russia. In the end it touched off a conflagration which may yet sweep across the entire world.

Six years earlier, in 1895, another paper bearing the very same name, the *Spark*, was started in Tortona by the newly ordained Don Orione. It was just a little news-sheet in which he wrote of the work which was already being done and of the far greater job that needed doing among the poor boys of Tortona. From the start the young Luigi had undoubtedly seen his future work as one that could spread and develop. It is doubtful whether he could foresee the role which his little *Spark* would play in it. In practice it did for his work precisely what Lenin's *Iskra* did some years later for that of the Bolsheviks. By 1898 it had become a little more ambitious in its size and make-up, and its title had been changed to "The Work of Divine Providence".

One day, by some means, a copy of this little periodical came into the hands of the Bishop of Noto, a Sicilian town of some 50,000 inhabitants. The Bishop read it, liked it and admired the work it described. So he wrote to Don Orione saying that next door to his own residence there was a large empty house. He would like Don Orione to run it, partly as an orphanage and partly as a juniorate for his seminary—a nursery-bed for priestly vocations.

Don Orione saw this as the hand of Divine Providence clearly intervening once more, and so he replied as quickly as possible. Before long the first small group of priests, whom he could ill afford to spare from those working with him, was sent off to Sicily. The Work of Divine Providence was no longer a purely local affair confined to the diocese of Tortona. From that first contact with Sicily big things were to grow. Indeed, the incident may be described as one of the major milestones in the progress of the Congregation and in Don Orione's own life. Its consequences were enormous.

But most of his time during these years was spent in and around Tortona. He was both rector and king-pin teacher in the main school, he had his agricultural school some miles away to keep an eye on, his work amongst boys was unending, and every week-end he was out preaching somewhere in the diocese. Everywhere his sermons drew large crowds and were exceptional both for their oratory, passion and delivery, and for their deep spiritual content.

*

There was, as was to be expected, a good deal of informality about those formative years of the Congregation. It had grown out of an urgent local need, but a need which was also universal. It had clearly been inspired by the influence of Don Bosco upon the adolescent Luigi who at that time consciously modelled his work upon that of the Salesians in Turin.

To some extent its fortunes, certainly until the new house was established in Sicily, were bound up with and dependent upon the will and pleasure of Mgr Bandi, Bishop of Tortona, a strong-minded man whose desire to support what he saw to be a useful work was tempered by a very proper caution.

A big step forward was taken when, on the Feast of St Benedict, March 21, 1903, the Bishop formally and officially gave his approval to the Congregation, under the title of the Work of Divine Providence. Patron saints of the Congregation included St Benedict, St Francis of Assisi, St Vincent de Paul, St John Bosco and St Joseph Benedict Cottolengo. Between them they reflect something of the scope of the work as it has developed over the years.

A far bigger step was taken in 1906 when Don Orione sought, and at once obtained, an audience with Pope Pius X. The Rule of the Congregation had been drawn up. Now he wanted it to have the Pope's approval.

He set off for Rome with high hopes. If he got the approval he sought, his work would henceforth be on a more stable footing. But he set off, too, with certain misgivings. He was anxiously hoping that the Holy Father had a short memory, for there was a skeleton in his cupboard about which Pius X already knew, if his memory was good, for it involved the Pope himself.

One day, whilst he was still a young seminarian, he had been walking down a street in Tortona when he met Joseph Perosi, father of the brilliant young musician Lorenzo. Lorenzo's aptitude for music had been noted by his Bishop while he was at the Tortona seminary for he had already started composing. When Cardinal Sarto, Patriarch of Venice (the future Pius X) started a choir school at St Mark's, Mgr Bandi recommended Lorenzo to him. So Lorenzo was sent to Venice to complete his studies there. The Cardinal spent much time discussing his music school with him and quickly grew to love him. One might have expected that his father, Joseph Lorenzo, would be a proud and happy parent. But he was a very worried one the morning Luigi met him in Tortona.

"Have you had any news of Lorenzo?" Luigi called to him across the street.

"Don't talk to me about Lorenzo," Joseph answered. "Things are bad with him, very bad."

"What has happened?"

"Just imagine it. The Cardinal Patriarch of Venice has made him his friend and he's spoiling the boy."

"What do you mean? You ought to be very proud."

"Every evening my boy has to go to Cardinal Sarto's rooms and they talk alone together and play cards. The Cardinal even offers him cigarettes. It's not good for a young boy like that."

Luigi agreed. He grew indignant at the thought of the Cardinal spoiling his old friend and fellow-Tortonese, and he was concerned at the old man's anxiety. So he went home and on the spur of the moment wrote the Cardinal Patriarch one of his impetuous letters; and it was not one of those that he revised. In it he sharply expressed his regret and disapproval at the great man's behaviour. He marched out of the house, posted the letter and then, having cooled off, said to himself: "My God, what have I done? What possible right has a young seminarian to reprove one of the great princes of the Church?"

For weeks he waited for an explosion which never came. Then he began to comfort himself with the thought that perhaps the Cardinal's mail was so heavy that he never saw one half of it. He heard nothing from Venice until just before his ordination when an anonymous parcel came with a Venice postmark. It contained a length of cloth—enough material to make a good cassock. Its sender had rightly guessed that he had no money with which to buy one for himself for the great occasion. Luigi, on opening it, thought that at least Lorenzo had not forgotten him. But he rather hoped that the cloth had not been bought with money won at cards.

Now Cardinal Sarto was Pope Pius X and Luigi was on his way to ask of him a favour which no one else could grant. The aid of Divine Providence was certainly required this time to see him through.

The Pope received him warmly and listened in a fatherly way to his description of his work and what he hoped to do. Don Orione produced his Rule which Pius X approved in full, after making some minor modifications and adding to the title the word "Little", so making the name of the Congregation "The Little Work of Divine Providence". This suited Don Orione perfectly, for it made his Congregation strictly Pontifical.

The Holy Father blessed the spirit and the aim of the work "with my greatest blessing". Widening Don Orione's own horizons and revealing the sort of future he foresaw for the Congregation, the Pope went on to say that he wanted the Founder "to work for the union of the Churches in the East". Then, after a few minutes silence, he added: "That is an undertaking of the highest order."

Emboldened by all this, Don Orione, having got so much, thought he would ask for a little more. So he reminded the Pope that what he was doing cost money, of which he was permanently short. The Holy Father at once arranged for him to receive a financial gift and promised further help.

He gave the young priest his blessing. When Don Orione rose from his knees Pius said: "Just a moment." He took his Breviary from the table. "I brought this to Rome with me when I came," he said. Don Orione stood wondering where the conversation was leading. The Pope opened the book. "Here inside it is something I want you to see." He passed it to Don Orione who at once recognised his own letter, the one he had sent as a seminarian.

"Even the Pope, you know," said Pius, "frequently requires to be reminded of the need for humility. For this reason I have kept your letter and have it with me all the time."

He gave Don Orione a quizzical look.

"By the way," he said. "Did you get the material all right for your first cassock as a priest?"

★

There was much in that first audience for Don Orione to remember. It was remarkable in every way.

According to one story, he arrived early for the audience and so decided to go to a nearby Carmelite church to pray. When he got there he noticed that confessions were being heard and, as he always begrudged wasted time, he slipped into the confessional to make his own.

The Carmelite hearing confessions was old, rather deaf, slow of speech, meticulous and strict. After each sin that Don Orione confessed he delivered himself of a long sermon. Orione began looking anxiously at his watch as the time for his appointment with the Holy Father approached. Finally, in desperation he cut his confession short and rushed to the Secretariat of State puffing with exhaustion.

"Don't worry. Be calm," a Monsignor told him. "Someone is still there, and although you are late it doesn't matter."

By the time the Pope was ready to receive him Don Orione had cooled off, but was still feeling frustrated.

Pius laughed as he approached him.

"You have arrived late," he said, "but I forgive you."

"I'll tell you another thing," he continued, "when you go to confession tell *all* your sins without worrying about the time, and end your confession calmly."

It was one of many occasions when Pius X revealed his ability to know things for which no natural explanation could be given. It was a gift which Don Orione himself was also to develop.

From the time of that first audience—which has been described as the dialogue between two saints—Pius X and Don Orione remained close friends. Each admired the other and each collaborated directly in the other's work.

Incidentally, Pius had taken as his motto, when he became Pope, the one which Luigi had adopted for his club in 1892 and which is now the motto of the Sons of Divine Providence: *Instaurare Omnia in Christo*—"Restoring all things in Christ."

CHAPTER V

Earthquakes: Physical and Theological

On the morning of December 28, 1908, nearly 100,000 people were killed when an earthquake hit Sicily and Calabria, Italy.

The news shocked the whole of Italy. All down the West coast of Calabria and particularly on the Eastern coast of Sicily around Reggio and Messina, there was chaos and human misery that seemed endless. Railways were out of action, postal deliveries ceased, contact with the outside world was reduced to a minimum. Troops were sent from Palermo to help to restore order.

When Don Orione heard of this enormous catastrophe his thoughts went at once to those who had been orphaned. His one desire was to get to the scene of the disaster to assist in any possible way. Maybe his own establishment at Noto could help. But getting to Sicily from North Italy was an expensive business. The little community in Tortona made a quick decision. A precious pair of oxen were sold and Don Orione, accompanied by another priest, Don Pasquale, set off. Don Orione went to Messina, Don Pasquale to Palermo.

When Don Orione arrived, soldiers and rescue squads were already engaged in finding survivors and getting out the dead. Tens of thousands were lying under the ruins. The disorganisation was such that rescuers and victims alike were sleeping in the streets. It was winter, and a cold wind brought new misery with it. For the first two days and nights Don Orione had neither food nor sleep, throwing himself into the work with no thought for himself. When the work of rescuing the living and extricating the dead was completed, the far bigger and longer task of organising relief for the homeless, the orphaned and the injured began.

The priest from Tortona became well known at Messina Cathedral because over and over again he dropped in there to pray. He was given a bed in the sacristy, but would offer it to the first person in need and then sleep on the floor. In the first grim days he had shown his spontaneous heroism, his compassion for those in trouble and his love of the poor. Now his exceptional qualities as an organiser began to be seen. The relief work was already in full swing when Mgr Emil Cottafavi arrived in Sicily on January 10, sent there by the Holy Father as Papal Delegate.

Don Orione at once offered his services. Before long he was busy getting orphaned boys into his own Congregation's house at Noto or having them sent up to another house at Cassano all' Ionio, in Calabria. A secular committee had been set up to organise the rehabilitation and relief work, but before long it was almost wholly dependent upon the little priest from North Italy. His services were later recognised by the Government who presented him with a gold medal. He was the only priest to be honoured in this way.

The Pope showed his gratitude by presenting him with Colonia Santa Maria for use as an orphanage; this was a house outside Rome which had been given to the Pope only recently.

He honoured Don Orione still more by giving him a job which called for a combination of exceptional strength of character, tact and charity.

The effect of the disaster upon the clergy in Eastern Sicily may be compared to the consequences of the Black Death in the Middle Ages. Many of the best priests had died. The survivors with the strongest sense of duty, the most selfless and devout, had died during subsequent tremors as they took the Blessed Sacrament to the injured and dying. Those whose first concern was for their own skins were among those who lived to see another day. Moreover, as in the case of other earthquakes and disasters of exceptional magnitude, a further effect was a general demoralisation, which the clergy did not escape. The sheer size of the job to be done and the apparent hopelessness of ever getting to the end of it tended also to defeat the weaker ones.

The result was a wave of indiscipline among many of the clergy. It grew to such an extent that the Archbishop of Messina himself asked the Pope to appoint a Vicar General from outside Sicily to get the situation in hand. His letter was taken to the Pope by a lawyer named Bersani, an active member of a Catholic charitable body. When he went to see Pius he found that he was not available. A Cardinal took the letter from him, read it and asked him his view on the proposal. Bersani had seen Don Orione at work and suggested that he was the man for the job as he had the advantage of already being on the spot and of knowing the situation. On the following day the Pope appointed Don Orione Vicar General. It was as unenviable a job as any priest could be given.

Here he was, a humble 36-year-old secular priest, with the authority to overrule, if necessary, men twice his age and of high position in the Church. He had been entrusted to do a job which had proved too big for the local Bishops. No job was ever more likely to bring a priest unpopularity and earn him the bitter hostility of his fellows. Throughout his life Don Orione showed the utmost loyalty to the reigning Pontiff and so, although his new appointment meant dropping his own work in Tortona and switching to a peculiarly uncongenial job, he did so at once and without question. Don Sterpi was left in charge of all the business to do with the infant Congregation, the expansion and development of which was brought practically to a standstill.

Don Orione's new job lasted three years in all. From organising boys and enthusiastic clerical supporters he had to turn to reorganising restless and demoralised priests and dealing with those who shared his cloth but not his views. As was to be expected, he made a great success of it. Everything which came from the Vatican had to pass through Don Orione's hands; all authority was vested in him. The situation, so far as the local Bishops were concerned, had got completely out of control. He held the reins. He brought down to Sicily one of his own priests, a canon lawyer and archivist, from Tortona to assist him. He persuaded the undisciplined clergy, where possible; where persuasion failed he disciplined them. He switched them to new work, supervised them and slowly began to get things back to normal. Where there was chaos he built up new organisation. But he did it at a price, for he learned what it was like to be hated by some of his fellow priests and even plotted against.

Some were so demoralised that they were prepared to stop at nothing, to stoop to anything, no matter how criminal nor how vile, in their determination to get rid of him. But he survived their plots, turned enemies into friends and earned the undying love and gratitude of Pius X.

The Holy Father knew of the difficulties which he was meeting and the hostility that was being shown to him. He had just appointed one of Don Orione's priests, Don Felix Cribellai, a Bishop and he entrusted to him a message to Don Orione, letting him know that no matter who might be against him he was with him.

"Tell Don Orione," he said, "to have patience, patience, patience, for it is with patience that miracles are worked."

When the effect of the earthquake had been overcome Don Orione asked to be allowed to return to his own work in North Italy which was needing attention. He returned enormously increased in stature, authority and prestige.

He returned, also, with yet another interest and mission. Whilst he was in Messina dealing with recalcitrant priests his troubles were increased by some of the Catholic intelligentsia, both clerical and lay, in the city, showing themselves strongly tinged with modernism. Pius X at that very moment was striking blows at modernism and the modernists. Don Orione tackled and overcame the problem, not by using coercion, nor by doctrinal argument, but by the charity of his approach.

When he returned to the North he continued this work, just as necessary there, and gave a great deal of precious time and thought to it. Whenever he heard of a priest in danger of being unfrocked, actually unfrocked or even excommunicated, he would seek him out. To him these were men in urgent need of especial love and understanding. He had the ability and the knowledge to argue with them had he wished. He did not do so. He did not believe that in these particular circumstances anything could be achieved by such means. If these men were in good faith then clearly they had already listened to and considered all the arguments. What was needed was love to prevent them from becoming soured and embittered, and still more love if they had already reached that state.

He travelled all over North Italy and into Switzerland, seeking them out and bringing them to his houses. Often he persuaded them to live with him. He would eat with them, share his time with them, give up his bed for them, with never a word of argument or any attempt to prove them wrong or the Church's position right. And over and over again this simple, practical demonstration of genuine Christian charity coming straight from the heart won them back. In some cases he quietly persuaded them to work among his own orphans.

The Holy Father had already given him permission to hear confessions anywhere. He now used this privilege for his own purposes and time and again created the right conditions for its use. Among those he brought back were famous preachers and theologians, men who were regarded as intellectual giants. During this period he was as likely as not to be seen at any time, anywhere, in the company of someone who had fallen under suspicion or who had recently been unfrocked. His houses were full of such men.

The work, like that in Sicily, called for great tact and understanding. It was also full of risk for himself and his infant Congregation. Before long there were ecclesiastics and others who thought that the unfrocked priests, who were to be found in every one of his houses, were members of Don Orione's own Congregation. The community must itself, they argued, be riddled with modernism or rottenness; or perhaps it was that they were an ill-trained ignorant lot. The stigma stuck for years; it had been knowingly risked and was borne uncomplainingly.

From that day to this the Sons of Divine Providence have made this one of their special works and still in almost all their houses in Italy there are men working in a secular capacity who once were priests and have been brought back to the Church, and others who are actually priests and are now members of Don Orione's Congregation.

Almost inevitably Don Orione himself became suspect too. It was one of many calculated risks he took at one time or another in his life—risks which sprang from a charity which went "beyond all the normal limits". He knew that he was vulnerable, that he laid himself wide open to misunderstanding. But knowing this never for a moment deterred him.

The day came when so many over-zealous people had charged Don Orione with modernism, because of his continual association with notorious modernists, that Pius X sent for him. The Pope had fought a great danger to the Church with vigour. He was determined to wipe it out root and branch. It was to him a necessary but unpleasant task in which a lot of people inevitably got hurt.

When Don Orione came into the audience room he sadly said: "They tell me that even you are a modernist."

Then, when Don Orione had explained what he was doing, the Pope told him to get down on his knees. "Recite the Creed," he said.

Don Orione began. But he said it with such obvious fervour that long before he had finished Pius told him to get up.

"It is clear," he said, "that you are all right. Go and do whatever you think is useful."

From then on, with the blanket approval of the Pope himself, he could work not only among the unfrocked, but among the excommunicated as well.

Pius never asked for details of this work which continued for years. When excommunication was inevitable, Don Orione sought them out, tried to arouse in them a feeling of contrition and helped them back to an acceptance of the Church's authority. He knew that Don Orione was almost certainly the intellectual equal of any of them but that he did not seek their intellectual defeat. He sought their souls and these he won by his great love.

So who was he to stop him?

*

On January 13, 1915, on the eve of Italy's entry into World War I, there came another appalling earthquake, claiming some 30,000 lives, this time in the district of Marsica, near Rome. Remembering Don Orione's work at Messina, the civil authorities asked him to come and assist with the relief work in Marsica. He needed no asking. To him, if there was exceptional suffering, the call was one which was personal and direct. Before he set out he made arrangements for three houses in Rome, including the one given him by Pius X, to be used as reception centres. The stricken area was under snow when he got there and conditions were as bad as they could be.

He at once threw himself into the work. His personal example and organising ability won him praise on all sides. On Mount Bove, 4,000 feet up, was a village which had been totally devastated. When he heard of it he at once motored up to it through the snow. He did what he could to help, and then collected six half-naked, half-frozen, hungry and injured children and set off with them back to Rome.

Wolves were roaming the snow-covered hillside and soon he and his party had five of them yapping and snarling around the car. Don Orione comforted the terrified children by telling them "how fond these big dogs are of us".

In his *Essays and Addresses on Philosophy and Religion*, Baron von Hügel writes: "When my eldest daughter, some eight months before her own death, succeeded in reaching from Rome the centre of the terrible devastation just then caused by a specially violent earthquake in the Roman Campagna, she promptly had her observation riveted by a most striking contrast. There lay before her the wreckage and the ruin, the apparently blind and stupid carnage inflicted upon sentient, homely mortals by sheer physical forces, gas and fire; and terrified villagers merely added to the cruel confusion. And in the midst of all this death and destruction moved about, completely absorbed in the fate of these lowly peasants, Don Orione, a secular priest, a man looked upon as already a saint from and for the humble and the poor. He was carrying two infants, one on each arm, and wheresoever he moved he brought order and hope and faith into all that confusion and despair. She told me that it made them feel that somehow Love was at the ultimate bottom of all things, a Love which was, just then and there, expressing itself through the utterly self-oblivious tenderness of this lowly priest."

*

Gaetano Piccinini was another of those rescued by Don Orione. He told me his story as we sat together in the deserted ruins of the Forum, in Rome, late one evening after the gates had been shut and the place was deserted. As he talked, he conjured up for me from his memory the scene of that terrible day of more than 40 years ago, when death struck so hard at Marsica.

The first big catastrophic tremor came at 7.30 in the morning, just as the 15,000 inhabitants of his home-town were starting their day. The 11-year-old Gaetano had just been sent down the road by his mother to the home of his married sister to borrow something which was needed for breakfast. As he went up the stairs to his sister's apartment on the first-floor landing he picked up the family cat, a large white one, and put it on his shoulder. The cat was unusually bad-tempered, clawing him without provocation. He was disturbed by its strange behaviour.

Then suddenly there was a roar. "It sounded like some terrible storm at sea." The ground trembled and all around him buildings collapsed. His sister's house, being terraced, was one of the few that stood, but interior walls, doors and windows fell in. A door hit him throwing him against a wall; but he was not hurt, for the cat on his shoulder had acted as a buffer. On top of the door was a pile of debris. Gaetano lay for a while terrified and wondering how he could get out. Then the cat saw some light, crept to the hole and made its way through. "If the cat can get out, so can I," he told himself, and did, after easing his way out bit by bit.

He ran out to the street. From where he stood he could see that his own home was in ruins. As he made his way crying towards it, he saw bodies lying everywhere. In particular he noticed that one was that of a very rich and somewhat extravagant townsman known as "Millionario", who lay, a terrible sight, with his head flattened on the road, his arms outstretched. On his fat fingers still glistened the great diamond rings for which he was famous. To this day Gaetano remembers the vivid impression which the sight made upon his mind. "They're all the same when they are dead," he told himself. "Rich and poor alike."

He passed, too, the body of his 19-year-old brother Dominico. Then he found his home a pile of stones. His father, his mother, every member of the large family to which he belonged, every relative he had in the world with the exception of one brother, one sister and an uncle, had been killed. He ran back down the street to his sister's home screaming "Mammy", "Mammy". As he crossed the road he took another look at "Millionario", whose body still lay outstretched. But the diamond rings had gone. Some human jackal had cut off the fingers to get them. "I was filled with more horror by this," he told me, "than by the whole of the rest of the scene."

Those were the conditions in which Don Orione was working. In all some 30,000 had died and there were many new-made orphans like Gaetano Piccinini that morning.

Gaetano stayed with his sister and her husband for a few days. The story spread that there was a little priest who was finding homes for orphans. In due course Don Orione called upon them and they agreed that since there would be no future for anyone in the town, Gaetano would be best looked after if he went back with him to Rome.

They set out that evening, Don Orione, Gaetano and another boy, travelling by train. Don Orione had already taken many other boys to his houses in the capital, including Ignazio Silone, later to become one of Italy's most famous writers.

Don Orione radiated love and consideration, although he was not demonstrative.

"There were no affectionate embraces—he just radiated kindness," Gaetano told me. "I felt that I had lost a father and mother, but had gained a new father."

Don Orione kept up a running commentary on the scene from the carriage window, to distract the two boys. As Gaetano grew sleepy he felt a large hand creep round his shoulder and draw him close. It came to rest under his arm. Sleepily he opened his eyes and saw that between the fingers of the hand inconspicuously was held a Rosary, and as he dozed off he heard Don Orione beneath his breath repeating "Ave Maria. . . ."

The 90-mile journey was slow, for there were bridges down for all the first part of the way. They reached Rome at midnight and went for the night to the Church of St Ann in the Vatican, which Pius X had some time earlier given to Don Orione's Congregation. There, Gaetano was put into a camp bed in the choir, along with others, to sleep.

On the following day he was taken to the house in Monte Maria, which Pius had given Don Orione after the Messina earthquake. Don Orione had already brought some 150 boys there and a similar number had been accommodated elsewhere.

"For ever after that night in the train," Fr Gaetano Piccinini, member of the General Council of the Sons of Divine Providence, told me, "I kept that same picture of him; always combining prayer with action, inspired by love, with no affectation, no smarminess, no bunk."

*

Another story of Don Orione's activities at the time of the earthquakes comes from Ignazio Silone, the Italian Independent Socialist, ex-Communist and world-famous novelist. Silone was a boy at the time. His entire family was wiped out by the disaster.

"It was only a few days after the earthquake," he writes. "Some 50,000 dead still lay under the mounds of debris. Rescue squads were frantically being organised to care for the terrified survivors, who lived near their shattered homes in makeshift shelters. It was mid-winter. New tremors and snowstorms threatened the survivors. During the night wolf-packs, attracted by the stench of dead bodies, would swoop down from the nearby mountains. Huge bonfires had to be fed continually to keep them at a distance.

"It was in such a setting that I witnessed a strange scene one day. A little priest, dirty and sickly-looking, with ten days' growth of beard, stood surrounded by a huddle of small children orphaned by the disaster and gathered up by him among the ruins of my village. He was looking for some means of transporting them to Rome, looking in vain. The earthquake had disrupted the railroad. No other vehicles were available for a journey of some one hundred kilometres.

"Then, suddenly, five or six automobiles appeared on the scene. The King and his entourage had come to visit the stricken area. No sooner had these illustrious personages alighted and walked some distance away, than the unknown little priest began to load the shivering waifs into one of the automobiles. There resulted a lively altercation between the little priest and the *carabinieri* standing guard over the machines. At length the commotion attracted the attention of the King himself.

"Calmly, the little priest turned to the King and respectfully asked him for the use of one of the cars to convey the orphans to Rome. The King gave his consent. I was standing a few feet away and following the whole scene with mounting stupor and admiration. And when the little priest, with his cargo of children, had taken off, I asked those around me: 'Who is that amazing man?' Someone answered me: 'A certain Don Orione.' "

Ignazio Silone, incidentally, was later befriended by Don Orione after he had been expelled from a school to which he had been sent when his parents and all his family were killed. Throughout the years when he was a Communist, Silone, though at that time a Marxist atheist and anti-clerical, retained his love and respect for Don Orione.

Characteristically, Don Orione never for one moment loved Ignazio Silone any the less for the fact that he wandered so far from the Church. Indeed he would see that as a situation which called for greater love, not less. That it was a very real and practical love is revealed by two other stories which Ignazio Silone told me about occasions on which he met Don Orione.

Silone had left the students' hostel in San Remo to which Don Orione had taken him when another Order had expelled him. Instead of becoming a priest, as Don Orione had hoped, he had gone right over to the other camp and was editing a Socialist youth paper. His life was hard and often he passed his nights sleeping in the Colosseum for want of the price of a bed. Sometimes he had to go without food, too. For three years, ever since he left the seminary at the age of 17, he had been in difficulties, but his pride had prevented him from telling any of his old friends.

Now it was Christmas Day 1920 and, as usual,

he had only a few *lire* in his pocket. Though he was without religion he still wanted to celebrate Christmas so he went into one of Rome's lowest and cheapest eating-places to get a meal.

When he had finished the bill was brought to him. It showed that even the poor meal he had had cost more than the three or four *lire* which was all he had in the world. The waiter demanded his old hat and raincoat in lieu of payment, and said he would hold them until such time as the balance was paid. Silone knew that that probably meant facing the cold Italian winter without a coat, and resigned himself to the idea. He had no intention of begging or borrowing.

As he passed the Church of St Ann, however, he recalled that this was one of Don Orione's churches. That in turn reminded him of the friend and helper of earlier years, whom he had disappointed and let down. He had seen him from a distance on the previous day coming from the station.

That meant that Don Orione was in town. On the spur of the moment he said to himself: "Now *there* is the one person whom I could go to without difficulty."

"I knew," he told me, "that although I had not seen him for two years and although he knew my Socialist views he would none the less understand me as no other person could."

He called at the presbytery and insisted that

he must see Don Orione. "I would never have done it with anyone else."

Don Orione heard his voice and at once came into the corridor to greet him saying, "I'm so very happy to see you like this on Christmas Day." Then, before he could be asked, he put his hand into his pocket and without so much as a glance to see what he had taken out emptied its contents into Silone's pocket. He had guessed that there must be some special need which had made Silone overcome his natural pride. Knowing that his action was bound to cause the youth embarrassment, Don Orione cut the conversation short with a brief goodbye and Silone left.

"I went back to the eating-place," he told me, "and to the great surprise of the proprietor produced the money, and he had to give me back my hat and coat."

His second story is of an episode years later in the middle '30s. Silone was one day travelling North by train. He was on his way to a Spain in turmoil and which was heading straight for civil war. On the way he left his second-class compartment to stretch his legs in the corridor. He was passing the crowded third-class carriages when he saw Don Orione sitting in one of them. They briefly exchanged a few words but Silone did not linger as, being a well-known member of the Communist underground, he had a price on his head and was travelling incognito. A few days earlier an attempt had been made on Mussolini's life and the country was being combed for Communists. But he told Don Orione, who was on his way to Switzerland to visit one of his houses there, where he was going.

When they reached the frontier, Silone walked down the platform with a porter carrying his two heavy cases. Don Orione had a strong feeling that his wayward friend might be recognised by the militia and shot. So he caught up with him and kept close on his heels until he was safely off Italian soil.

"I kept near him," he explained later, "because I thought that they might shoot at him. If they did they might get me and that made it less likely that anything would happen to him."

CHAPTER VI

The Big Little Work

GRADUALLY, over the years, the Little Work of Divine Providence took shape and form as Don Orione developed his various activities amongst the scorned and rejected. It was enough for him to realise that an exceptional need existed anywhere, for him to want to tackle it with his all-conquering weapon of love. He described his work as follows:

"As it has been started on behalf of the poor, its activities must, if its true end is to be attained, be centred among working-class populations, preferably in the most wretched quarters of the great industrial cities. It exists for the poor and flourishes among the poor and the humble. Its members labour among the poor by work and example and by the perfect sacrifice of their lives made to Christ through love for the salvation of their brethren. Love is its field, but it by no means excludes truth and justice; on the contrary, it finds truth and justice through love.

"The Little Work exists to serve and to serve with love. With God's help it intends to live on, in order to practise the works of mercy for the moral and material well-being of the most abandoned. Its slogan is the *Caritas Christi urget nos* of St Paul, and its programme is Dante's 'Our love has no closed doors'. Therefore it welcomes and embraces all those who are in sorrow, all those who cannot find anyone to give them bread, to offer them a bed, to bring them comfort. It becomes all things to all men in order to bring all to Christ."

From his earliest days as a boy with Don Bosco he had known that such work requires organisation; equally important, that organisation must depend upon the sacrifices of utterly devoted, dedicated people, prepared to go anywhere and do anything in its service.

The organisation associated with the work grew up around his own personality and activities. Those who came were usually either first captivated by him as a person and then drawn into his work for the poor, or else heard of the work and were attracted by it, and then, having met him, came under his spell.

It began with the modest boys' club meeting unofficially in the cathedral tower, and then later officially in the Bishop's garden. Next came the school and the agricultural college. Priests and seminarians of the most diverse types were attracted to the work and to the spirit of charity which underlay it, until, with Don Orione as their leader and the driving force behind all their activity, they became the Sons of Divine Providence.

Leo XIII, in 1898, welcomed and encouraged his plan for a small nucleus of Hermits who would support the visible work with hidden prayer and simple toil of a type that would be but an extension of that prayer.

It was Pius X who extended the work into broader fields than Don Orione had ever visualised. He never at any time sat down and drew up a blueprint of the organisation and its work. It was an organic growth, stimulated and directed at one point and another by successive Popes.

It was Pius X also who approved and amended his Rule and who helped to name his organisation. The anti-clericals in the early days of the school in Tortona used to refer jeeringly to Don Orione's boys as "the Pope's little army". It was a title of which he was proud.

In 1906 Don Orione went to tell the Pope that he would like to respond to an appeal he had received to send some of his members to Patagonia, in Argentina. He had been offered by an Archbishop an immense and promising region in which to work. The Pope was sympathetic; but he had other work in mind for him at that moment and he knew that the Sons of Divine Providence were still limited in number and so could easily take on too much at once. Don Orione had visions of his Congregation taking root and spreading in a new continent. Pius told him of work right there on his own doorstep, which he would like him to undertake.

"There is another Patagonia," he said, "just beyond St John's Gate. Many of the people there are Christians only in the sense that when they were little they were baptised in the Church of St John Lateran. But apart from that everything is lacking." He was referring to the population of 10,000 inhabitants who had moved into a new suburb of villas, wine shops, places of entertainment and great mansions—but no churches—just outside Porta San Giovanni in the Via Appia.

Don Orione had gone with high hopes of obtaining a field of work capable of rapid expansion. The whole thing had been quickly switched to something quite different, but he did not come away depressed. For the Pope himself received his perpetual vows, telling him that the witnesses, in the absence of others, would be "our two guardian angels".

Don Orione's comment was: "I confess that this Papal audience was not only full of grace and joy for me, but I feel also that it has quite renewed me in Christ and encouraged me in the service of the Church since it has left me with a keener and stronger desire to consecrate myself wholly to love God and to sow in the hearts, especially of the little ones and of the poor, the sweet love of God and of the Pope. O the ineffable consolation enjoyed by those who stand humble and faithful at the feet of the Church and of the Apostolic See!"

No dashed hopes here!

Don Orione got to work evangelising the suburban pagans outside Rome. He sent some of the best of his priests for the work. The Pope provided a beautiful church for the new parish.

In any case, by November 1914 Don Orione's first missionaries were sailing for Brazil. There they established their headquarters in Mar de Espanha. Don Orione had his foot inside another continent. He had been called there because his work corresponded so exactly to the needs of the day. And he had got a big new parish and church from the Holy Father, into the bargain.

All through his life that was how things went. He would see, or be told of, some pressing need. He would respond to it. Then there would be difficulties, opposition and possibly a temporary switch to other work. But before long the original project would be under way, and on far more ambitious lines than he had ever dared to dream of.

The Messina earthquake and the troubles growing out of it, which led to his being pitchforked into work that was certainly not of his seeking, revealed his unsuspected ability to handle difficult situations with energy, superb tact and skill. It revealed in him also a native shrewdness which, like so many other of his qualities, could as easily have been used for evil as for good. When Don Orione was charged with modernism in a letter of denunciation, Pope Pius simply passed it to him and said: "I wanted to show this to you so that you shall know with whom you have to deal," adding that he should take care whom he trusted. To this Don Orione replied: "Don't worry about that, Holy Father; I think I know how to use my wits and sometimes it seems to me that I would have made a good policeman. Anyway, bless my cunning, that I may always use it to good ends." The Pope's answer was one which Don Orione took literally. "Go ahead, go ahead. Continue to do as you have done up to now. Go right to the edge, but be careful not to get pulled over. Apart from that I know that there is no danger."

From that day on the Sons of Divine Providence have gone 'right to the edge'. They have lived on the edge; treading where more cautious men, but ones who are less aflame with love, do not dare to go.

*

In 1904 Pius X entrusted to Don Orione's Congregation the chaplaincy of the Church of Sant' Anna dei Palafrenieri in Rome. He promised Don Orione that he would build a big church for him, one that was to become the parish church outside the Gate of St John. The Church of All Saints, consecrated under Benedict XV, was in fact built on the land given by Pius X.

In 1911 the Holy Father suggested to Mgr Misciatelli, who intended to offer the Holy See the agricultural colony of St Mary of Monte Mario, that he should present it to Don Orione, who had several years before established his hermits and priests there and now had many orphans there too. This was the Pope's "Thank you" to Don Orione for the trouble and sacrifices suffered at Messina, where by commission of the Pope he had held the office of Vicar General.

Pope Pius and Don Orione had much in common. Both were of working-class origin. Both had a great love of the poor. Both cared most for those whom the world thinks matter least. The consequence was that it was not long before a genuine personal friendship existed between the two. From his earliest days Don Orione had been a 'Pope's man'. For him the Holy Father was indeed the Vicar of Christ on earth. But the relationship which grew up between them was such that when they met, the tone was one of familiarity, cheerfulness and spontaneity. In such an atmosphere his work could thrive and flourish.

*

The type of work which the Sons of Divine Providence were doing would clearly benefit if it were supported by a women's order. So in June 1915 on the Feast of St Peter, he founded the Little Missionary Sisters of Charity. The Institute was at first simply a new branch of the Work of Divine Providence, but after a few years the situation had to be regularised and they became a recognised Order with their approved new name. Their work, like all the other things Don Orione did, simply grew, almost spontaneously, out of an obvious need.

Don Orione had been to see a noble family in Genoa. There he met a beautiful young 23-year-old girl, Josephina Faldetaro, who impressed him with her great natural kindness. He had for some time intended to gather together some sisters to help him. He invited her to found with him a women's congregation. Josephina objected that she was too young, too inexperienced. Under Don Orione's pressure she gave in. He fixed a date and in due course she turned up in Tortona, smartly dressed in the most fashionable clothes of the day. She was every bit the nobleman's daughter, spirited and cultured. She was joined by the second member of the Order, a 40-year-old cook who had a crippled shoemaker brother who came to live with them. The three of them moved into Don Orione's original schoolhouse. The house had been left deserted, filthy and full of rubbish by the last tenants. Josephina asked Don Sterpi, who had been appointed to be their spiritual adviser, "What shall I do here?" Don Sterpi replied: "The first thing is to do some sweeping and cleaning."

Josephina went home again some years later, but by then the women's Order was founded. By 1917 they already had their own novitiate and some 20 nuns.

Don Orione intended that they should have no distinctive habit. He told them that clothes were of no importance, it was the work that mattered. He wanted nothing that would cut them off from the mass of the people, most of whom, particularly in San Bernardino, had wandered far from the Church. In practice, the very absence of a habit defeated its own purpose. As the 'nuns in mufti' went around in ordinary dark clothes the populace suspected them, demanded to know what they were doing and charged them with prying into other people's affairs. The windows of their convent were broken, their garden was destroyed. The hatred, deliberately fanned by the Marxists, grew to a point where their life threatened to become impossible. Moreover, the women themselves, contrary to what Don Orione had expected, wanted to have a distinctive habit. Early in 1918 they blossomed out with one which he had himself designed.

The nuns began in 1915 with a kindergarten and a girls' club. Then they started work amongst old people. When Don Orione founded his first orphanage they were brought in to assist. Soon it was clear to them where their work lay: their mission, like that of the Fathers, was to the poorest of the poor. "For the rich," Don Orione told them, "God has provided already. You just go to the very poor."

*

When an Italian work of charity begins by including the word 'Small' or 'Little' in its title you may be fairly certain that it will not be long before it is immense.

St Joseph Benedict Cottolengo, for instance, 150 years ago called his work in Turin the "Small House of Divine Providence". Today it is the biggest concentration of Christian charity on earth, and the title sounds almost like a pious joke.

It is a fantastic city within a city: a city of

suffering. To the Catholic, brought up to see human suffering in its proper context and to discern its spiritual meaning, it is breath-taking as a colossal demonstration of Christian charity in action. To the non-Catholic it must in a sense be macabre. The total volume of suffering there is incalculable. To those without God it must look from the outside like a City of Dreadful Night. Yet over it all breathes the spirit of charity, of sacrifice and of suffering offered up for spiritual gain.

This huge place was never planned, it grew naturally. There are whole streets of hospitals and sanatoria; asylums for the insane, the blind, the maimed, the horribly deformed, the orphaned, the rejected; and, of course, convents, monasteries and churches. In one sense the place is one great monastery.

Some 6,000 people live there as patients. They are tended by members of religious Orders, male and female, who give their lives to the work among this world's flotsam and jetsam. There are some 1,000 nuns of a dozen different Orders.

Members of one Order devote the whole of their time to the washing of soiled linen which comes from the beds of the diseased, the incontinent aged and the uncontrolled insane. They launder seven tons daily.

There is another whose members tend the insane. When I visited the Cottolengo I went into a ward in which hopeless and helpless men were being fed. A tiny nun was spoon-feeding a man who roared incessantly, purple in the face with rage as she ladled gruel into his open mouth.

Another Order, the Sisters of St Vincent, provides the nurses who look after the patients in the hospitals, sanatoria, and homes for old people. Yet another tends the deaf and dumb.

And then there are the Carmelites. They are cloistered and bound to silence. They go barefoot and do penance all day in their convent for those whose sins have been responsible for the infirmities of so many of the patients. They pray for the success of the work and for those who suffer. They support the whole great edifice, as it were, with their prayers.

Similarly, there are Orders of men, priests and lay brothers, which supply the male nurses and attend to the mentally sick.

To the Cottolengo go life's rejects from every part of Italy. Only two qualifications are required of those who apply for admission and free maintenance: that they be sick or deprived, and that they be poor.

Don Orione had been inspired in his youth by the work of Don Bosco among the street boys of Turin. But, in that same city, he also saw this great work that had been begun by St Joseph Benedict Cottolengo, and was profoundly influenced by it. It was that influence which made him spread his frontiers from his original idea of boys' clubs and schools wider and wider until, like the Cottolengo, they embraced everyone who was in dire and peculiar physical need.

In fact, his frontiers went in time beyond the limits of the Cottolengo itself, for they included those in special spiritual need as well, such as, on the one hand, unfrocked priests, among whom he developed a particular apostolate and on the other, street girls. He went 'right to the edge'. On one occasion he told one of his priests in Venice: "I would put my finger into hell to reclaim souls."

As his work for the sick poor, the cripples, and the mentally and physically deficient, developed and grew, the peasants of North Italy began to call his establishments "little Cottolengos". No greater compliment could have been paid to his work, and Don Orione, who had a great devotion to St Joseph Cottolengo, fully appreciated it. The title today has official Papal recognition.

*

The number of his houses grew and grew. As often as not they came to him without his asking for them. Thus, for example, he had wanted the work to spread into the Archdiocese of Venice but there seemed no opportunity to get his foot inside the door.

A secular organisation named the Congregation of Charity, publicly financed but run in co-operation with the Church, had two houses in the city. One was used as an orphanage, the other as a place for all sorts of needy boys. The organisation became a victim of the wave of industrial unrest which came to Italy in the years following the end of World War I.

During a strike of all the municipal employees in the city the lay workers of the Congregation's two houses stopped work, too. The Cardinal Patriarch asked Don Orione if he would take over the second one because the boys had been left unattended. Don Orione at once moved in some of his priests to take on the work. The first thing he did was to abolish the locked punishment-rooms at the top of the house. He turned them into play and work rooms, to the indignation of the strikers who said that this would mean the end of all discipline, but to the delight of the boys.

The Sons of Divine Providence ran it so successfully during the strike that they were asked by the Cardinal and the municipality to continue the work. They have remained in charge ever since and are still financially assisted by the municipal authorities—a unique situation. Both houses were already endowed by past benefactors.

In 1921 the second house came to the Sons as well.

★

A request for help which at once struck a chord in Don Orione's heart came in 1921 from the Patriarch of Jerusalem who invited him to start an orphanage and agricultural centre there. The sentimental appeal of working in the Holy Land was irresistible. The Patriarch had formerly been the parish priest at the Church of St John Lateran in Rome and whilst he was there had got to know the dynamic little man from Tortona.

Don Orione quickly sent out a small group of his priests accompanied by one of the Hermits, who took over a big settlement at Rafat, 13 miles from Jerusalem. The land, which was owned by the Church, was divided into some 50 family smallholdings. The Arab settlers lived on their own holdings but were directed by the small team of priests. Wheat, maize, beans and apricots were grown and the whole project was fully mechanised. There was, however, a failure to agree about the administration of the orphanage which went with the settlement. This ultimately led to abandonment of the project.

A second settlement was started at Capernaum, near the Hill of the Beatitudes. There the idea was to have a scheme which would improve the land, provide a livelihood for peasants and accommodation for pilgrims. But this scheme, like the first, proved unsatisfactory and in 1927 the last of the priests came home.

To the end of his days Don Orione regretted having to leave Palestine, and the Sons of Divine Providence still plan to return there some day.

★

Another call to which he responded came in 1925 from De Lago on the island of Rhodes. There for a time the Sons ran boarding schools, an orphanage for refugee children from Armenia and an agricultural centre.

This enterprise came to an end in 1949 when a defeated Italy had to return the island to Greece and the priests, because they were Italians, met with hostility from the newly liberated Greek population.

★

In the summer of 1921 Don Orione set out for Brazil carrying a special diplomatic passport given him by Pope Benedict XV. He had from the start been attracted by Latin America and believed that there was great work to be done there for both bodies and souls.

When he went out his missioners had already been working there for seven years and he wished to see their work and also to look into the chances of extending it.

By the time he returned to Italy the following year, he had visited Uruguay and Argentina as well. In all three countries he found a big welcome awaiting him and an almost unlimited need for his work. During his stay he opened new homes at Rio de Janeiro and São Paulo in Brazil and at Victoria in the Argentine, and paved the way for the establishment of his work in Uruguay.

The mission in the Argentine in particular quickly spread. He already had a friend, who later died a Cardinal, in the secretary at the Papal Nunciature. It was he who had invited Don Orione to the country. He offered him several houses for the care and training of street boys. Don Orione sent to Don Sterpi, who had remained in Tortona, a request for a few priests. Soon five were on their way. He stayed with them for six months until their work was securely established there. It has been said that what Paris was to Don Bosco, the Argentine was to Don Orione; it was the place of his greatest successes.

In South America, too, he found that there was a need for his work among unfrocked priests. In Brazil he gave a retreat for nearly 100 of these men who were so near and dear to his heart. Many came back to the priesthood or to the practice of their Faith as a consequence. When he got back to Italy he told a member of the Sons of Divine Providence that the trip to South America would have been more than justified had he found only one such priest and brought him back.

For the next 15 years Don Orione was mainly preoccupied with consolidating his work and deepening his own spiritual life.

Members of his Congregation were now spread all over Italy, in the Dodecanese, Palestine and South America. Before long they were going into Poland, Albania and the United States.

The expansion into Poland is of particular interest in view of the fate of that great Catholic country today. Like Belloc and Chesterton, Don Orione held the view that Poland was of immense importance to the whole of Christendom.

The first Polish vocation—he was later the Congregation's first Bishop—came to Rome as a pilgrim. In those days many Poles came on foot or cycled across Europe to the Eternal City. Most of them were attended, when they got to Rome, by a Polish Jesuit who was a friend of Don Orione's. When the Jesuit found that in one batch of pilgrims there was a young man who wished to become a priest, he sent him to Don Orione who gave him an especial welcome. Before long other vocations were coming from Poland and the Congregation was quickly established there. There were the usual works of mercy, a big agricultural centre, churches and a mission among the people living in a shanty town near Warsaw. Don Sterpi visited Poland once, but Don Orione, who longed to go, never managed to get there.

The story of this branch of the Sons of Divine Providence is one of sacrifice and martyrdom. Some of the priests died in Dachau, victims of the Nazis. Others gave their health, and one his life, nursing the sick during a typhoid epidemic in Warsaw, where the Sons had one of their churches.

When World War II broke out a number of the Polish priests and seminarians were stranded in Italy. They longed to go back to their motherland in her hour of need, but were unable to get there. Most of them never got back. Some now work in South America. The coming of Communism to their country at the end of the war made return impossible.

As a token of his especial love for Poland, Don Orione hung a great Polish national flag in his room in Tortona, which was still there at the hour of his death. It hangs there to this day. But Don Pensa, the present Superior General, told me when I talked to him in Rome that reports of what remains of the work of the Congregation in Red Poland now come only very irregularly to the superiors.

Don Orione's priests have been allowed to continue their work in their churches but their schools, orphanages and agricultural centre have all been taken over by the State and are now made to serve the cause of Communism. Determined that the youth, tomorrow's citizens, shall be theirs, the Communists refuse the Fathers any right to work among them.

*

From being a local diocesan Congregation in Tortona the Congregation had by the mid-twenties become one which reached across the globe. The Sons of Divine Providence and the Little Missionary Sisters of Charity sought vocations wherever they could find them. But a natural process of growth had begun, too. The orphanages and schools yielded their crop of young postulants. The work was becoming known and appealed to boys and girls with high ideals who came to join it. The twin Orders had their flourishing seminaries and novitiates from which went out a stream of dedicated men and women.

To support them in their work Don Orione in 1927 started yet another Congregation, which at that time was the only one of its kind in the world. It consists exclusively of blind nuns. At first they lived in the Little Missionary Sisters' mother house in Tortona, but after a house had been found for them and a Little Missionary Sister of Charity had been found to help in their direction, they were installed in their own convent in San Bernardino.

I never found a happier, more serene group of women anywhere in the world than the Blind Sacramentine Sisters whom I visited in their Convent in Tortona. Dressed in scarlet and cream habits, they spend most of their lives in prayer and simple work of a type which they can do despite their disability. Today they have two Italian houses, the one in Tortona, the other in Central Italy. There is a third in the Argentine. They pray unceasingly for the Little Work of Divine Providence and those engaged in it. And they pray, too, "for those who do not pray".

★

What of Don Orione's own development in these years? A priest in Venice, who went to his seminary in 1922, told me that by that time all the boys regarded him as a saint and so did many of their parents. The boys' one worry was that he set his own standards so high that they feared that they would never be able to live up to them.

Those who come from the Piedmontese countryside affirm that by that time, too, his name was already a legend throughout the region. And around it had inevitably grown up a mass of folklore, mainly concerned with the miracles which he was said to have worked. But his own simple illustrations used in the pulpit in the early days when he spent every week-end preaching in the Tortona diocese lived on too. One which the peasants to this day recount with relish is how he told them: "I and my work are like the engine of a train. When it starts it is all puff, puff, puff"—in Italian 'puff' means 'debt'—"and so is my work. But once the train has got going it runs quickly and easily and the puffs cease."

Another priest who first met Don Orione in 1927 said that he still looked like a shepherd, simple, and obviously of humble origin. To the end he kept that same appearance. Yet he was able to mix easily in any society and appealed to intellectuals and peasants, noblemen and workers alike.

In his devotions he was still childlike. Those who encountered him at his prayers heard him repeating his *Aves* slowly, word by word like a little child who has just learned them and to whom they are still too fresh to be slurred over and gabbled. His favourite prayer was the *Paternoster*. But all his life was a prayer, and the pious ejaculation which came most naturally to his lips was "Jesus, my Jesus".

Before he set out on any journey, or started any new job, he recited an *Ave*. If a letter of importance was being despatched he would ask whoever was going to post it to stop first at the chapel and say a prayer for its success. He believed absolutely in the efficacy of prayer, resorting to it and expecting results from it, in the manner of a housewife who turns on an electric switch in order to do her cleaning or cooking. Through prayer all things became possible to him.

His devotion to the "Santa Madonna" remained as childlike, simple and heartfelt as his prayers. He was at his happiest when he was organising some colourful procession to a shrine of Our Lady. In 1928 he arranged a pilgrimage from Tortona to Caravaggio, near Milan. Nearly 800 people travelled the 90 miles by train. With Don Orione were three or four of his priests. They had a busy day before them so they had an early supper together, then at 9 o'clock each took a mattress from a pile. Don Orione helped to arrange the others on the floor, then, since there was no floor-space left, he put his own on the table. They settled down for the night.

When everything was quiet he whispered to one of them: "See if the others are asleep." They were. "Come with me," he said. They went together to the church and on the way told the women pilgrims who had not yet gone to bed, that they would hear their Confessions. The stream of penitents went on for hours. When the last woman had been shriven, Don Orione left the church with his companion. He turned to him and said: "In that building over there the men are lodged. Make some noise outside it so that they wake up, then tell them that if they wish to have their Confessions heard they should come to the church steps and I will hear them. They are sleepy and so you must sing hymns and loudly recite the Rosary to keep them awake." A queue formed and Don Orione heard one Confession after another until dawn. He went to bed at 4.30 in the morning, just before the Angelus. Then, when the others got up he rose too. When one of his unsuspecting colleagues asked him if he had had a good night, he gave an enthusiastic affirmative, whilst silencing his companion of the previous night with a glance.

He spent much of his time in the junior seminary, for his love for boys never grew less. And always they fell under the spell of his personality. This was so imposing that the smallest and apparently most insignificant word from him lived on in their memories. Thus, for example, one priest to whom I talked said that his greatest moment was one night when Don Orione walked through the playground filled with postulants. The boys were playing a particularly noisy game which might well have irritated him. Instead he said very simply: "Buoni, buoni" ("Be good, be good"). The incident seems trivial enough, but he said it so sweetly, and in such a fatherly way that the two boys who heard it swore to each other that they would follow him to the ends of the earth. The priest who told me of the incident still thought of it as one of the big moments of his life.

Don Orione retained over the years his belief in the usefulness of the unexpected dramatic action. Often those actions, simple in themselves, would make a lasting impression on the minds of others, not least because coming from anyone else they would have hopelessly misfired or would have been resented.

For example, during an annual retreat for priests at the Villa Moffa, near Turin, he found two of his priests who despite the character of the occasion were sitting at ease on a comfortable old divan in the sun far too long after their mid-day meal. They had clearly not caught the spirit of the retreat. Indignantly, he sent for them, scolded them in front of the entire community, and ordered that the divan should be burnt in the yard there and then and that the two priests who were by now contrite should recite the *Miserere*. "I have done this," he said, as the divan went up in flames, "so that you shall remember for ever that we are not meant for a life of comfort."

That same idea underlay his remark made on another occasion to a group of seminarians: "We of the Little Work are the wheelbarrows of

Divine Providence." He believed that the work amongst the most humble of men calls for exceptional humility and for a readiness to be used by Divine Providence for the most menial of tasks.

Another example of Don Orione's love of the dramatic action is one of which the Tortonese townspeople still talk with wonder—and with a chuckle.

On a hill outside the ancient town, established by the Romans, are the remains of a medieval castle. All that is left of it today is the tower. Some of the 12th-century castle was destroyed by Frederick Barbarossa. Napoleon destroyed some more. But the ruined tower, some 60 feet high, still stands securely locked so that no one shall complete the work of demolition.

For a long time on a certain day each year a procession had gone through the town carrying a statue of the Madonna. Then the practice was allowed to lapse. Don Orione wanted to revive it. There were those who warned against it. Tortona had always been a Marxist stronghold and even under Mussolini continued to be a centre of Socialist and anti-clerical activity. Those taking part in the procession might be publicly abused or even attacked. Moreover the Fascist authorities were not sympathetic to processions other than their own.

However, in 1931 Don Orione organised and

led a procession up the hill to the castle. It was understood that there would be nothing in the form of a demonstration. The people would walk with their statue to the old tower, light candles, pray briefly and then disperse.

The procession was orderly, and no opposition came. The candles were lit and the prayers said.

Don Orione looked at the assembled thousands and thought of the opportunity that was being missed. The crowd said one last prayer and was about to disperse, when suddenly they were startled to hear a great voice booming out above their heads. Through the dusk they saw Don Orione, high up on the top of the tower, holding above his head a great Crucifix for all to see. Somehow he had pierced the defences, scaled the great locked gate and climbed the 60 feet to the top.

Away across the valley down which flowed the river Scrivia, beyond the town, and opposite to the hill on which the crowd was gathered, was a vineyard-covered range of hills towards which the wind was blowing. Don Orione had always had a powerful voice which he could throw with amazing skill. That night the wind helped him. So did the hills which stretched right down to the Po valley, for they acted as a sounding-board.

The consequence was that not only were the thousands assembled on the hill treated to a powerful, extremely moving and challenging extemporary sermon, the townsfolk far down below heard it, too. Those who sat at home in their doorways pricked up their ears as they heard the oration from above. They went out into the streets telling others as they went. Soon every street corner had its knot of incredulous listeners. Then Don Orione climbed back the way he had come and the procession, singing exultantly now, made its way down the hill, through the town and so home.

The incident was not only the talk of Tortona that night in 1931, it remains so to this day.

He was himself, as he was bound to be, aware of the power of his personality and he used it to get the men and the things he wanted. One priest told me that when he was aged 30 he was a market porter and salesman. One day Don Orione passed his grocery stall in the *piazza*. He stopped, came back and looked at it, and then at the salesman whom he summed up at a glance.

"Why aren't you a priest?" he asked.

"Because I got tuberculosis during the Great War and because I had only an elementary school education."

"That doesn't matter. Come with me and I will make you a priest. I'll make you a porter of Divine Providence."

And that was that. The man left his market stall there and then, became a priest and was later at Don Orione's death-bed as one of his most trusted followers.

*

The same fiery temper and turbulent temperament that had made Don Orione claw at other boys in rage as a child and had later made him over-punish the boy in his first school, were still apparent in later life.

Once when a group of seminarians, old enough to know better, were interrupting his work, he stormed into their room with blazing eyes. "You scum" (*vigliacco*), he shouted. He disappeared into his room, still fuming, and slammed the door behind him. Before long a very humble, chastened Don Orione came back. With an enormous sorrow which entirely cancelled out his anger of a few minutes earlier he said, "Forgive me." Then, pointing to his tongue he shook his head and said, "This tongue of mine, this horrible tongue of mine."

No man ever understood his own nature better. His father had fought with Garibaldi, he had grown up with a natural admiration for the rebel and he knew that he was a natural rebel at heart. He once told the boys at the seminary: "If Christ had not kept his hand on my head I would have been a revolutionary." To realise how true that was one has only to recall his great sensitivity to human suffering and to injustice, his tempestuous nature, and his natural hatred of cant, and to remember that the period in which he grew up was one in which all these things were driving the working class of Italy and elsewhere away from the Church and into the ranks of the anti-clericals and the Marxists.

When I asked Ignazio Silone if he had ever met anyone who shared Don Orione's temperament he said without hesitation, "Only one man: Lenin. I have met no one else of the intellectual stature of those two men, combined with the same magnetic and rebellious personality and the same immense drive. Don Orione might easily have been a Lenin." Ignazio Silone was Italian representative on the Communist International in its early days and knew Lenin well. His life as a revolutionary, a great and respected literary man and, today, as a Social Democrat Deputy, has brought him in touch with many men. And he knew Don Orione well. It was against that background that he made this comparison.

It was no part of Don Orione's job to dabble in politics, but there was no escaping the impact of the Mussolini régime. While he was quite prepared to number some of its supporters and backers among his friends and the benefactors of his work, he would not compromise with them on the abuses of the régime. Once when he was particularly incensed at something that Mussolini had done, he exploded: "If I did not wear this cassock that man in the Palazzo Venezia would not be there, even if I had to lead an army against him myself." Those who knew him believed that that too had its particular point and one of which he was fully conscious. He was a natural demagogue. That characteristic might have taken him far in Fascist politics. Backed by the forceful character and intelligence of a Lenin it might even have led to his pushing the dictator out of the Palazzo Venezia.

It might also quite easily have led him, as a well known priest with a great potential public, into the trap into which some popular 'radio priests' have fallen in recent years. But like his temper, and his turbulence, he re-canalised his demagogy and used it for the glory of God and the service of souls.

CHAPTER VII

Troubles and Triumphs

GETTING his work established in countries on the other side of the world was often easier than getting it into dioceses on his own doorstep.

At home there were all the well-established vested interests one expects to find in a country where the Church has been established and highly organised for many centuries. Even those most zealously occupied in works of charity and mercy may still be jealous of others engaged in the same or similar forms of activity. And the jealous are not always over-scrupulous as to the methods they use.

To go into some huge area of South America where hardly any form of Catholic organisation existed was relatively plain sailing. To get the work into Turin or Milan, for instance, which already had well-established charitable bodies, orphanages, asylums and schools was far more complicated. Yet no one could pretend that these provided help for all who needed it.

There were still plenty who needed the aid of the Sons of Divine Providence. There was no necessity for anyone to imagine that they had the right to a monopoly in good works. Yet, human nature being what it is, this was one of Don Orione's greatest obstacles to development in Italy in the 1930's and probably caused him more worry than anything else.

*

Genoa is one of the richest cities in Italy. It is also one of the poorest. Its busy port and its many lovely houses creeping up the hills that fringe it present at one and the same time a picture of industry and of gracious living. But behind its beauty there is ugliness and squalor; its busy docks conceal the hopelessness of the unemployed and unwanted.

That combination of wealth and poverty had made the Archdiocese of Genoa famed for its works of charity. Within its borders there have always been good people with both the wealth and the will to aid good causes, and near at hand there have been poor people in plenty to prod the consciences of the complacent. Working in the diocese in the '30s were some 100 religious charitable bodies of varying sorts. Orders and

Congregations were attracted to it not only by the great scope there was for work amongst its poor but also because of the support which they knew they could get for their work.

Cardinal Minoretti was a good man, keenly interested in these charitable efforts and presiding personally over many of the organisations responsible for them. He was also a man of strong character, sometimes impetuous but always just. When Don Orione approached him for permission to start his work among the poor the Cardinal resisted. It was not that there was any personal antipathy between the two men. Each admired the other. But they differed on what seemed to them to be the best interests of the people of the city.

The Cardinal did not want to see the number of organisations added to. He did not want them treading on each others' corns. Nor did he want the work of well-established bodies which were functioning usefully and well to be disrupted by jealousies and conflict. Moreover there were so many of them that, with an economic depression developing, they were already complaining of lack of funds. "This new work may grow to big proportions," he said, "and what will be the effect upon the others?" He insisted that he had a great admiration for Don Orione. "He is a holy man," he said. "But I am unsure of the wisdom of allowing him into Genoa."

So when this much talked of Tortonese asked if he might come, the Cardinal, with the best of intentions, made clear his disapproval. Don Orione argued that the times were such that if you took in one beggar another immediately appeared at your door and that, therefore, his work was needed. Local jealousies should not be allowed to stand in its way.

In the end he got permission to go ahead, but it was a grudging permission and often the Cardinal would hesitate when Don Orione needed his aid.

Once inside the diocese, as the Cardinal had half feared and Don Orione had hoped, the work went forward by leaps and bounds. None of the local clergy knew of the stresses and strains behind the scenes, and they supported it with enthusiasm. Don Orione, who went straight to the poor and abandoned, fired their imagination and drew a response from all that was best in them.

"I come to collect the rags—the rags of your society," he told them; and despite all obstacles he broke through to Genoa's generous heart. From a small seed there quickly grew a big work. Today the Little Work of Divine Providence has in Genoa more houses and works of mercy than anywhere else on earth, and certainly the biggest show-piece of all—the most modern of hospitals for the treatment of mental disorders.

*

Milan was a tougher nut to crack than Genoa had been. The magnificent marble cathedral, with its 100 slender spires, its 3,300 statues and its great bronze doors, is the city's very heart. It has an appeal which is irresistible to all who see it. But to the Milanese people it is the 'Madonnina', the great statue of Our Lady, perched high above the roof and looking out across all Milan, which is their darling. The Madonnina beckoned and called to Don Orione.

Milan, with its great Catholic past and its present-day masses of semi-paganised industrial workers, was a challenge to him. He waited for an opportunity to establish a house there, no matter how small, from which he could spread out. As usual, the opportunity came.

In Milan was an old Carmelite convent which had been in use since the Middle Ages. In 1933 its community of nuns, who for long had been impoverished, suddenly found their fortunes vastly improved when an elderly Sicilian Princess joined their ranks. Both she and her husband had longed to end their days in the religious life and so, by agreement, they separated. The old Prince became a monk, the Princess a Carmelite nun. Each brought their riches to the Order of their choice.

It was not long before the Princess Paterno had been made superior of the old convent in Milan. At once she began to think along more ambitious, and businesslike, lines than the other nuns had ever dared to do. She decided to get rid of the tumble-down convent and the valuable land which went with it and to use the money to get a new and better place. She asked for the convent half a million *lire* (which in 1933 was a considerable sum) and wanted 600,000 *lire* for the land, which could be used for development and which she was prepared to sell separately.

Don Orione heard that the property was on the market; he wanted it and so he proceeded to deal with the Princess. The only thing he lacked was money. He simply had none at all. But he did know that he wanted very much to start work in Milan. He talked to her of future payment, and of loans. The Princess wanted hard cash. She had no confidence in Don Orione's ability to pay and she was determined to have her hands on the money before she parted with a single brick of the property. When Don Orione left she thought she had seen the last of him. He travelled to Tortona planning just how he was going to use the convent.

That same evening, in Tortona, a Piedmontese woman recently back from South America and proud of the reputation of her fellow Piedmontese, met him in the street.

"You look preoccupied," she said, "what is worrying you?"

He told her about his desire to have the convent in Milan, and mentioned the fact that he had literally no money at all.

"I will lend you the half-million lire," she said.

He promised to pay her back when he could, but pointed out that he could not say when that would be, since he depended entirely upon the generosity of others.

Years later, on December 7, 1938, the foundation stone of the biggest building of the Sons of Divine Providence was being laid in the grounds. Don Orione was there, so too was the good lady who had lent him the money—which was still not returned.

She walked over to Don Orione.

"I'm glad to see your work is progressing," she said. "I would like to see it prosper. Here is my contribution towards it." As she said it she passed him a receipt for half a million *lire*. It was not for nothing that people called him "God's bandit".

But much had happened between the making of that loan and the passing back of the receipt. In the first place, there was the question of the land which Don Orione badly wanted. The convent was useful—it is still used as a home for the Fathers serving the great "Cottolengo" nearby —but it was the accompanying land which held out the hope of big new development in the future. He raised the matter with the Princess, urging her not to sell it separately. She held it for him for some time, saying that if he could produce the 600,000 *lire* it was his. Finally, she grew impatient. One day she told him that if she was to proceed with her own scheme she must have the sum in full by 3.0 p.m. that same day. Otherwise she must sell it to someone else.

As Don Orione came out from the interview he met a priest friend to whom he outlined the situation.

"I've sent a message to all my houses to the effect that in each a priest must at once be appointed to watch before the altar and keep up a continuous battery of prayer," he told him. "Now let's go and have some lunch."

As they talked they went into the former convent in which the first priests were now established, through the study and into the dining room. As they did so a seminarian stopped Don Orione.

"There's someone in the reception room who wants to see you," he said.

Don Orione apologised to his companion and told him he would be away for not more than five minutes. Approximately five minutes later he came back, clearly only half-conscious of where he was. His thoughts were far away. The other asked him what had happened. From his inside pocket Don Orione extracted an envelope.

"I told you I wanted 600,000 lire before 3 o'clock," he said. "Divine Providence has sent it along. That man handed me a cheque for exactly that sum. We must now go to the chapel and thank Providence for what has been done, and then we'll go and have our lunch. We'll have better appetites for it now."

The night the land became his, he hailed a passing motor driver and asked him to drive him slowly around its boundaries. "It's all ours," he said, "and I want to see every inch of it."

That side of the task of getting established in the Archdiocese of Milan was relatively easy. There was another side which worried him much more. The same kind of jealousies and ecclesiastical suspicions which he had encountered in Genoa he also met with here. And they were not as easily overcome.

In the study of the old convent he once looked out over the newly acquired grounds and prophetically told a friend: "One day this will be a huge place and foreign tourists will come to see the cathedral, the palace and this."

But there were times in 1933 and the years that followed when it seemed doubtful whether he would be able to remain there at all. Opposition from established bodies who regarded his field of activity as their monopoly came near to hatred. They calumniated him, they smeared him, they protested to Cardinal Schuster, and they sent letters of protest to the Vatican about him. They persuaded the Cardinal that the arrival of the Little Work of Divine Providence in his Archdiocese would rob him and the existing Congregation of vocations. Don Orione would get money which would have otherwise come to them. They alleged also that his priests were an ill-trained ignorant lot. This last allegation was one which he had met before. It sprang from a belief that the many unfrocked priests who were to be found in and around his establishment were members of his own Congregation who had gone off the rails.

Complaints went to the Holy See in such numbers that Cardinal La Puma, who was in charge of Religious Congregations, also began to ask: "What are we going to do about this man and his Congregation?"

Don Orione was utterly convinced that he was right in wishing to extend his work to this great industrial city. But the charges and accusations hurt him deeply none the less, and his health began to be undermined by constant worry.

When an invitation came in 1934 to return to South America and to attend the International Eucharistic Congress in Buenos Aires, he accepted willingly. The work in South America was going forward without hindrance and he wanted to see it developed still further. There was, therefore, every reason why he should go. But without doubt he was also weary of the fight, or rather of the character of the fight, in Milan. He wanted to breathe a different, more encouraging atmosphere. He wanted also to deepen his own spiritual resources, which had recently been taxed to the full. "I am going," he told an intimate friend, "in order to escape religious persecution." But outwardly he was serene.

From the start the trip was an enormous success. He was not going to the Congress as an official delegate but was invited to travel on the same boat as those who were. The ship was packed with Cardinals, Bishops and high ecclesiastics of one sort and another, among them the Papal Legate, Cardinal Pacelli, later to become Pope Pius XII.

On the way out it was agreed that each night they would all gather to hear a sermon. One evening Cardinal Pacelli was chosen to preach. But as Papal Legate to the Congress he was more busy than most and had at the last moment to ask to be excused. With practically no time for preparation, Don Orione was invited to take his place. Few men have preached to a more august assembly of Church leaders or a more critical congregation. He had with him no works of reference, no sermon notes. But he took his audience by storm with a sermon which drew on all that was best in Italian Christian literature.

It was interspersed with long quotations from memory, with exact references.

His stock was high by the time he reached the Argentine.

★

In the Argentine there was no friction. Everything he touched went well and was appreciated. He loved the Argentinos and they loved him. When he preached in Italian these Spanish-speaking people flocked to hear him. The similarities in the two languages, and his ample gestures and vividness of expression, enabled them to understand him.

For three years he laboured night and day to make the Little Work of Divine Providence known and to assist the development of its activities. When he arrived the Congregation had only two small houses, but new ones were soon springing up everywhere. What particularly impressed the Argentine working class was the fact that all his work was for the needy who had traditionally been the most neglected.

He took charge of the famous Marian shrine of Tucuman and spread an intense devotion to the Madonna wherever he went.

He travelled out to the leper colony at Chaco to bring hope to the hopeless there. He started a network of schools which are today responsible for the education of some 6,000 children.

Just outside Buenos Aires he established his first "Little Cottolengo" in South America. It takes the form of 18 separate small units built on a huge piece of land and between them covering almost every type of charitable activity.

He travelled to Chile, to Las Pampas and to Brazil. Wherever he went he left behind a trail of new foundations. He burned with a new energy, a new hope. He was determined to spread his work of charity far and wide. And he burned himself out.

In Brazil he started a mission to the Indians. Today the mission works among a purely Indian population of 50,000 nomads who live in a vast area two-thirds the size of Italy, nine hours' flying distance from Rio, having no means of contact with the outside world other than the aircraft.

He started many works of charity too, although the Little Work of Divine Providence has never developed in Brazil on the spectacular lines that it did in the Argentine.

It was his intention when he went out to South America, to give a great impulse to the work there. He achieved far more than he had ever dared to hope.

Three times President Justo, of the Argentine Republic, who had a great personal love for him, visited Don Orione's houses as his guest. He was present for the laying of the foundation stone of the "Little Cottolengo" in Buenos Aires, and when Don Orione left he received from the President who came down to the quayside, a signed photograph, and from his wife a magnificent bouquet of flowers.

His health was poor throughout this period and the doctor absolutely forbade him to fly. But he flew across the Andes none the less.

The Argentinos sought him out wherever he went. All day and every day they gathered outside any place where he happened to be staying, waiting to bring him their troubles and to seek his help. They brought him their children, too, and he blessed them; their lame and their blind, and he found them homes; their possessed, and he exorcised them.

During these years he gave himself, and wore himself out, to such an extent that those around him grew alarmed and wrote to tell Don Sterpi that he must find some excuse to coax him home.

Nobody guessed, as he went from one job to the next, that he had left behind him in Milan a crisis which still continued and still weighed heavily on his mind. Men who worked closely with him in South America during that period have told me that they saw no sign of short temper or irritability. He was always joking, serene and as near to being relaxed as a man of his temperament was ever likely to be. He suffered in silence and shared his mental suffering with no one.

There was still trouble in plenty in Milan, but

there was good news, too. From all over Italy vocations were coming to the Congregation in such numbers that Don Sterpi had opened a new seminary to accommodate 300 in Bra.

Don Orione's departure from Argentina was an occasion which those who witnessed it will never forget. The Cardinal was there to see him off, together with all the foremost State officials. And the common people were there in their thousands, many of them weeping as his vessel sailed away.

★

The Milan to which he returned was all too much like the one he had left three years earlier. His presence, and that of his Congregation, was resented by the various vested interests of piety who considered that he and his work were a threat to themselves and their work.

As soon as he got back, the same representations began once more to be made to Cardinal Schuster. The priests in the house of the Congregation in Milan were depressed by the atmosphere in which they lived. They were under constant fire from prominent lay Catholics, particularly from one group which claimed that Don Orione's activity merely duplicated their own and overlapped with it.

Don Orione was planning a multi-purpose "Cottolengo" in the Buenos Aires style, which would help every sort of human reject. They objected to his building it, to the name of his Congregation, and to the name which he proposed giving to the establishment. They were personally known to the diocesan authorities. Don Orione was not. Their complaints were therefore not unnaturally heard with greater sympathy and so led to opposition from the diocesan administration itself.

On one occasion some of his opponents sent to him a deputation of protest. He pointed out that as the Cardinal had already approved his work they were in no position to oppose it. Left with not a leg to stand on, they insulted him. Once upon a time his reaction might have been volcanic. But during his years in South America he had brought himself under control and he took their insults without a murmur. It was not easy. As he travelled back from Milan to Tortona that night he did not read his breviary, nor did he spend his time, as he so often did, writing innumerable letters. He sat for a long time silent and withdrawn. Then his companion heard him say to himself: *Soffrire e tacere e adorare* ("to suffer, be silent and adore the will of God"). He said it three times. Then, with the tension eased, he became his usual companionable self again.

He was still as outspoken as ever. Once during this period, when the discussion had come round to the bureaucracy of the Church, he startled his hearers by roundly declaring: "I would like to see the Vatican spending some of its money on a small town of charity which would be a model of Christianity in practice, built right beside St Peter's, so that people coming from all over the world would see the works of charity!"

One of his earliest and most faithful supporters was the wealthy Senator Cavazzoni, who had represented Italy on a League of Nations International Narcotics Commission at Geneva. Cavazzoni stood by him through all his troubles, believed in him and sought to get him accepted by the monied class to which he himself belonged. Don Orione could not develop his work without their financial support. They were its potential benefactors. But it was precisely that class which suspected him most. To these cultured people he was just a self-educated peasant-priest who had managed to get into the public eye. Cavazzoni clung to the view that if he could once get them to meet him or to hear him they would be won over.

He founded a group of the "Friends of Don Orione" composed of his most intimate associates, to discuss how the break-through might be made. Together they hit on a brilliant idea. They would arrange for him to lecture on Divine Providence at Milan's great Catholic university.

The Catholic University of the Sacred Heart has more than 8,000 students and is the very centre of Italy's Catholic cultural life. It is now, as it was then, presided over by Fr Gemelli, a scholarly and much respected Franciscan who was once a Marxist atheist.

Started in 1921, the university had grown rapidly and in 1932 it took over a neighbouring 15th-century building. Here was the hall where Don Orione was to lecture. Once a Benedictine monastery, the building adjoins the church of St Ambrose, under which the fourth-century Saint and the city's two protomartyrs lie in state. The hall was once the monks' refectory. In a less godly period Napoleon stabled his horses there, and as late as 1924 it was being used as a barracks.

It is a superb hall. Its ceilings are covered with magnificent paintings. During one of the many plagues of long ago, these paintings were white-washed over, along with the rest of the building, as a means of disinfecting the place. They have since been cleaned and their colours restored. The walls of the hall are decorated with great pictorial panels. On the one behind the rostrum from which Don Orione lectured is a great painting of the Wedding Feast at Cana dated 1545. The 950 seats rise in three great tiers. It has 'atmosphere', and its acoustics are superb, as I know from having tried them.

The hall was crowded for Don Orione's lecture. Many, if not most, of those who filled it had come to hear Don Orione expose his own ignorance.

All intellectual and middle-class Milan was watching his performance. Almost from the moment that he opened his mouth he had their attention. It was not long before he had their respect too. For this self-taught peasant-turned-priest gave a lecture which is still remembered as one of the best and most erudite delivered in that famous hall.

Don Orione had a great love of Italian literature and in particular of Dante. The way in which he drew on the Christian literature of their own country for his illustrations delighted the Milanese intellectuals. He quoted long passages from memory, cast new light on others, illuminating them in ways which had never occurred to them. The breadth and depth of his reading and understanding astonished the crowd and they were generous enough to show their delight. He made them see that what he and his followers were trying to do grew naturally and inevitably from all that was best in Italy's Catholic history, traditions and culture. By the time he had finished his lecture he had them in his hand. As he stepped down from the stand people crowded around trying to speak to him. Humbly, he excused himself. "I must go. I am in a hurry," he said. "I bless you all."

The press next day reported his success at length, and in superlatives. He had stormed this stronghold of resistance at precisely the level which it had least expected of him, and he had succeeded. He had conquered Milan. "He could, if he wished, be a professor of Italian literature," the surprised and delighted Milanese declared.

But he had done more than score a personal triumph; he had made his work acceptable. Nor had his appeal been only to heads, he had also touched hearts profoundly. Senator Cavazzoni had worked hard to get "anyone who was anyone" there. His wife, too, had helped to do the same. Amongst those she had persuaded to be present was one of Italy's youngest and most promising professors. He was brilliant. But he was an atheist, son of a well known anti-clerical. The professor attended the lecture and as Signora Camelia Cavazzoni watched his face she saw that he was becoming increasingly interested. At its conclusion, when the departing Don Orione blessed the crowd which was trying to mob him, the young professor went down on his knees with the rest. Later he told his wife: "There is something about that priest which makes him unlike the others." A few months later he was taken seriously ill. He sent for Don Orione who gave him the last Sacraments. He died reconciled to the Church and reconciled, too, as only a good Christian can be, to an early death.

*

The work was now established in both Genoa and Milan. Everything depended upon making more and more friends, among the poor who could be helped and among the rich who could help them. So Don Orione began a practice which continued until his death and which undoubtedly hastened its coming. Each Tuesday he travelled by train from Tortona to Milan, put himself at the disposal of anyone who needed him and then travelled back late at night.

All day long, regularly each week, a queue waited to see him: children with their own small problems, old people looking for a home, the physically sick seeking healing, the spiritually sick seeking his aid, the rich seeking favours or coming with gifts, the poor coming to bless him or to seek the sympathy which no one else would give them.

A man needed a home: Don Orione would try to get him fixed up. Another would tell him how he had not been near a church for 40 years: Don Orione would hear his confession. A rich nobleman would pass him a packet containing money: he would pocket it unopened. If the next man happened to be someone in need, the packet would be passed to him, still unopened. So it went on all day. It was exhausting work, but it was a million times worth while.

He did that every Tuesday in Milan. Every Thursday he did precisely the same thing in

Genoa. All over North Italy there are people today who were helped by him in this way in those last years of his life. They remember with gratitude each word of his, they recall each glance he gave them. It seemed almost as though he knew that his time was short and that he must give everything he had got.

Those who associated with him over the years compare the Don Orione who went to South America in 1934 with the one who returned in 1937. They say that a great change had taken place. He was more at peace with himself. It was not that the lion had become a lamb, nor that it had even been tamed. It was just that the lion in him had been brought under control or, to change the metaphor, those elements of his nature which were potentially most dangerous had been redirected.

By nature he was fiery, rebellious, tempestuously strong-willed, impatient, unconventional, virile, vivid—all these adjectives were used by the most diverse types from peasants to prelates and professors with whom I discussed the matter. When he returned from South America and during the remaining three years of his life it was as though all these things were controlled for God and against himself. He had always known what he wanted, and he had always been determined to get what he wanted done. That was still so, but what he wanted was now what Divine

Providence wanted. That had not always been so.

He returned from South America a sick man. His heart, his liver, all his internal organs seemed weakened and worn out by constant overwork. For years he had been a diabetic, using insulin. Now he had many other ailments, too. Although still only in his middle sixties, he carried himself like an old man, walked like an old man, found the steps of Rome Central Station a burden and hurried only with difficulty. Yet the old fire was still there. When he wrote his letters in his great scrawling handwriting the sound of the steel nib tearing its way across the paper could still be heard in the next room. He still showed all the old dynamic energy. But now it had to drive along a worn-out, protesting body.

That the old lion still lived was demonstrated one day just after his return. He was sitting at his table writing. On to the paper fell a narrow shaft of sunlight coming through the keyhole. Suddenly the light was cut off. Don Orione noticed it and he knew what it meant. He had sought privacy, yet some young seminarian was peering through the keyhole. Without warning he got up, sent the door flying back and burst into the corridor, throwing the youth on the other side against the wall as he did so. Then he went quietly back to his room and continued his writing. But that was the last outburst of that type. In the years that followed the fire still burned, but it burned only for the cause to which he was so patently giving his life.

In those last years he showed himself able, to a remarkable extent, to understand other people's failures—even those of ecclesiastics which he had always found most disturbing and had been able to suffer least patiently in the past. He always found charitable explanations and excuses for the weaknesses of others. He had none for his own.

CHAPTER VIII

Malcovati's 'Miracle'

DURING his lifetime and still more after his death, the Italian faithful credited Don Orione with miracles of the most diverse types. They said that he had the gifts of prophecy, healing, exorcism, even of bilocation.

When people who had known him, people in all walks of life and at every cultural level, told me about these things, I neither accepted nor rejected their stories. It was not for these that I had come to Italy. Incidentally, after his beatification cause was started, the Holy See, which is not easily satisfied on such matters, accepted some at least of the stories as authentic. Frankly, so far as my own personal inclinations were concerned, I was not particularly interested in them.

But there was just one private miracle that I wished he would work for me. Over and over again as I travelled the length and breadth of

Italy, visiting all the main centres where he had worked, talking to everyone I could find who had ever known him, I heard the name of Malcovati. Time after time it occurs, spelt out in block capitals, in the note-books which I was filling one after another.

Malcovati was said to be a notorious anti-clerical who became a great supporter of Don Orione and a benefactor of his work; an immensely rich man, high up in the Fascist régime but behind the scenes—a man with immense power, who became Don Orione's humble but anonymous disciple. Knowledgeable people recalled that on big Fascist occasions he had been seen among the V.I.P.s, but always in the background. They also remembered that he had worn in the lapel of his coat a badge which read: "In the event of sudden death I do not wish to have the Sacraments."

As an example of Malcovati's influence with the authorities I was told by the Superior of one house in Genoa that he was much hampered by the fact that no made-up road came to his hospital. Somehow Malcovati got to hear of this, had a word with the municipal chiefs, and a new road was built within a few days.

In Genoa I heard that one Thursday in 1938 the usual long queue of mixed types was waiting to see Don Orione when a man was noticed standing among them who was quite unlike the rest and whose face seemed familiar. He was a big, expensively dressed man who carried himself like one accustomed to being obeyed. That in itself was not unusual, for there were generally some of Don Orione's rich supporters in the queue. But it was his face which was different and which made others stop and look. It was described to me as a naturally arrogant face. Moreover, it was said to be a curiously evil one. Yet he stood there humbly in the long line of old men and little children, beggars and benefactors, quietly waiting his turn. Every Thursday without fail, from that week on he was there until Don Orione could go to Genoa no more. Don Orione himself never talked of him.

The name of Malcovati in time became a challenge to me. I felt I had to see him and get his story. But, I was told by the Sons of Divine Providence themselves, Malcovati had disappeared from the scene completely either just before or just after Don Orione's death. He had been seen no more at their house in Genoa where Don Orione held his 'sessions', nor had the public seen him anywhere else.

Towards the end of my task of assembling the significant details of Don Orione's life I was beginning to feel that there was little hope of meeting Malcovati. The thought irritated and disturbed me. It seemed that here was something which genuinely belonged to Don Orione's story and yet was going to be absent from it, since I wanted no second-hand material in it.

Don Orione had for years the extraordinary good fortune—or you may call it a Providential gift—of being able to get the things he needed most. If he wanted half a million *lire* by 3 p.m., he got them. If it was urgently necessary that he should meet some particular person, the probability was that that person would turn up just at the right moment. This gift seems to some extent to live on among his closest followers. Between them they seem collectively to be blessed with all his various unusual qualities and characteristics.

I wished that he would grant me just one thing that I needed—and give me the opportunity to meet Malcovati, if he still lived.

Then one night I was on the station at Florence waiting for the late express to Rome. My companion, Fr Piccinini, had gone to buy some food and wine for the journey. When he came back he was just about to pass me my share when he said "Excuse me", and excitedly dashed across to a big man who, carrying no luggage, was making his way through the crowd. For a few minutes they stood talking together. Then Fr Piccinini came back, bringing the other with him.

"This is Signor Malcovati," he said.

The Rome train came in and we got in together.

"Do you mind if I travel with you?" I asked.

"No. If you are going to Rome, I'm going your way but only about half the distance. I shall get out further down the line."

I told him I was collecting material for a life of Don Orione whom I understood he had admired and loved. I told him too how I had been hoping to meet him more than anyone else, and had been fearing that I would not. I showed him his own name on page after page of my note-book.

"I have heard all sorts of garbled stories about you, your life and your conversion," I said. "Would you care to answer my questions so that I may have your story from your own lips and so get it straight?"

Malcovati told me to go ahead.

As I asked my questions I observed him against the background of the stories I had been told. Mario Achille Malcovati was an elderly man, big and with a figure which still conveyed a sense of immense power. His voice was so deep as to be almost a growl. This was an impression which was strengthened by the way in which he talked through almost closed lips. The cast of his face was still arresting and vaguely disturbing. I could well understand why people had thought of it as evil. One could still think of it as suggestive of evil, but it was the echo of evil rather than its reality, for it also now suggested resignation.

It was in 1938, Malcovati told me, that he first got to know Don Orione, and the circumstances of their meeting explain what followed. A friend of Malcovati's, an old man who all his life had been not just anti-clerical but anti-Catholic, lay very seriously ill. When his family tried to persuade him to allow a priest to visit him he resisted stubbornly. Then someone suggested that he might be willing to see Don Orione and the sick man agreed that this was a priest whom he could respect and that he would not turn him away if he came.

But Don Orione was in Tortona, miles away. They got in touch with him and he agreed to come if they could provide a car, since there was no other means of doing the journey. The only friend with a car available of whom the family could think was Malcovati, the bitter anti-clerical. So they asked him, as an act of friendship for the sick man, to pick up Don Orione and bring him over.

He agreed to do so, but only as an act of courtesy. Almost all his life he had opposed the Church. As a child he had known his father to be against the Faith, although his mother practised it. At the age of six he had made his First Communion to please his mother, but from his adolescence on he had followed in his father's footsteps. So when he was asked to go to fetch Don Orione he replied: "Why go and fetch a priest for a sick man who has done without until now? Why not leave him in peace?" But he was persuaded that this was really in accord with his friend's wishes.

Even so, when Don Orione got into the car he told him that he was wasting his time. "All his life this man has rejected your Faith," he said. "He will not accept it now. He is dying. You will not get him." Don Orione replied confidently that the man would not die yet and in any case he was not going to force his religion upon him. He went into the house and emerged two hours later.

"What happened?" Malcovati asked.

"Oh, he's all right. He received the Sacraments," Don Orione replied. "And he wants me to come again. I would like you to drive me."

Malcovati was impressed by the outcome of the visit, but he was all the more determined that Don Orione should not get him. To please a friend he would drive Don Orione over as often as he liked, but he was not going to be persuaded by this man or anyone else.

Instead of dying immediately the old man rallied, as Don Orione had prophesied. He was taken to a convalescent home at Lucca in the mountains. Every month for a year until the man died, Malcovati drove Don Orione there. As they travelled together the priest would talk of his work. Gradually, Malcovati became interested in it. He had been a philanthropist but had never helped Christian causes. He began to help Don

Orione with money and in other ways also. But he insisted that this had nothing to do with Don Orione's beliefs, only with his works.

Their road took them over the high Bracco mountain pass. On the way Malcovati would regularly stop for a rest from driving. Don Orione would use the opportunity to go on to the mountainside and pray. One night the other watched him and was moved to speak.

"I will accept the idea of God," he told him, "and I will help the poor, but I *will* not go to confession. I will not submit in this way to Rome."

Don Orione did not argue with him. His only comment was: "You are a just and honourable man. Remember, charity is the purest form of religion. You are charitable, so you are religious, too."

This was not what Malcovati expected. It took him off his guard. Don Orione sensed his mood.

"You don't want to confess to a priest," he told him. "Good enough. Kneel down at my side, ask God's pardon for all you have done wrong and I will give you absolution."

The proud Malcovati knelt down beside the little priest on that spot high up in the mountains and in the twilight wept like a child. When he got back to Tortona with Don Orione he received his second Communion. His first had been many years ago when he was a child.

"What in Don Orione," I asked him, "first appealed to you?"

"Being what I was, it was his strength of character that appealed to me the moment I met him," he said. "He had a great simplicity and yet he had great strength too. Later, it was his charity."

Then Malcovati told me a little about himself. He had, he said, been an industrialist and he left me to assume that as such he had backed the Fascist régime. It was because of this, presumably, that he had his legendary 'pull' with the authorities. But after his conversion by Don Orione, he gradually dropped out of public activity and devoted his time and money to assisting the Little Work of Divine Providence. In the end he gave away almost all he had, leaving himself only enough to live a very simple life. He left the city and his past behind him and settled unknown and anonymous on a small farm which he worked single-handed "somewhere between Florence and Rome". There he spent all his days, never leaving the farm.

"When did you last go to Florence?" I asked him.

"Not since I went to the country in 1940," he said. "I avoid cities and crowds."

"Then why did you travel up to Florence today?"

"Frankly, I don't know. Suddenly this morning I thought I would go there and so I travelled up."

"What did you do when you got there? Did you do any business? Did you go shopping?"

"I simply did nothing but walk the street. I bought nothing. As you can see I am empty-handed. When I had had enough of wandering about I went back to the station and there I met you."

Having known Don Orione, he seemed to take it simply for granted that he should have set out in this inexplicable way, since it was clearly in the interests of Don Orione's work that I should meet him and get his story. Such occurrences were a normal part of Don Orione's everyday life.

*

In Rome I found the son of the old man whose own conversion had led to that of Malcovati.

His father, who had held a high position in the civic life of Genoa had, he said, had a lifelong intellectual dislike for the Church. He was not a fighter but none the less was so deeply convinced that his own position was right that he made it openly known.

The reason why Don Orione's name was suggested when he was dying was interesting. The son, who for many years was not a practising Catholic, had been at one time Mayor of Genoa.

As such he was one day giving a public lecture when he saw at the back of his audience a little priest whose eyes never left his face. He found the eyes so penetrating, so disturbing, that they put him off what he was saying. When the lecture was over he enquired the name of the priest and was told that it was Don Luigi Orione. He never forgot him and everything he subsequently learned about him strengthened his conviction that here was a man of exceptional character and sanctity. Thus it was that the name of Don Orione was thought of when all else had failed.

When Don Orione entered the house, the son told me, he "came like a conqueror". He was completely master of what was, after all, a delicate situation. He introduced himself to the 77-year-old sick opponent of the Church like an old friend. "Years ago when you were the stationmaster of Genoa you knew my father," he said. And he recalled the exact circumstances in which they had met.

The old man was at once captivated by him. They remained alone for nearly two hours. Then Don Orione left. When the sick man's family returned to his room he said not a word. But his face was wet with tears. Neither did Don Orione tell the relatives, who were agog with curiosity, what had happened. He respected the other man's feelings.

The old man remained in the convalescent home at Lucca for 12 months. At the end of that period he weakened and sank into a coma from which he emerged on the night of December 24, 1938, just as the bells in the village announced the coming of Christmas. He died listening to them. All his life he had been outside the Church and because of his illness had still not been inside one when he died.

In both cases, that of the old man and that of Malcovati himself, Don Orione seems to have used the same approach as he used with the modernists whom he won back to the Church, and with the many unfrocked priests whom he befriended. He did not argue with them. He made no attempt to defeat them. He simply radiated Christianity and practised Christian charity before their eyes.

CHAPTER IX

"*To Die Standing*"

LATE one winter's night as Don Orione came from the station in Tortona he was stopped by a beggar. The beggar was in rags. Don Orione was wearing some new trousers which someone had bought for him. He looked at the man shivering on the roadside for a moment, then took him into a dark doorway. A few minutes later Don Orione was furtively making his way home through the back streets with only his underpants under his cassock. He was exhausted from one of his long days in Milan. He was ill. And by the time he got home he was very cold.

It was no isolated incident. For much of his time he was going around in shoes with holes in them, the former possession of some beggar with whom he had exchanged his own. Hats, coats, trousers, shoes, he gave them away without a thought to those who urgently needed them.

What, a doctor in Rome who had known him

well asked me, can you do with a man like that? The doctor had been an admirer of his life and work. He knew him well enough to be aware that any advice which he might as a medical man give him would go unheeded, if it got in the way of what he knew to be his life's work. Don Orione was what he was, and it would be useless and, indeed, wrong to try to prevent him from giving himself completely.

"It was typical," he told me, "in those last years after his return from South America for me to find him dog-tired, utterly worn out. Yet you could see him rally his strength by a great act of will when there was some chance of doing good to a human soul. The effort he made on such occasions exhausted him still further, it shortened his life. But it was God's intervention. What, I repeat, can a mere doctor do in such cases?"

His diabetes had not been serious before he went to South America but after his return it got much worse. Once a doctor friend in Genoa insisted upon giving him prescriptions for four different sorts of pills and medicines. As soon as he had gone, Don Orione looked at the handful of prescriptions in dismay. "If I took all these I'd have no thought for anything else," he said as he threw the prescriptions out of the window.

He was constantly taking risks with his health and putting an unbearable strain upon his already exhausted body. For years he had gone to bed after midnight, then risen at 4.30 a.m., and he continued to do this even when he was manifestly worn out. It was inevitable that a crash would come. It did.

One day in April 1939, he had gone over to Alessandria, a town not far from his home at Tortona. A priest of the Sons of Divine Providence was taking him over by car to visit one of his big institutions for boys, when he had a stroke. He was taken to a local hospital in a serious condition. The Bishop of Alessandria came to see him. Priests and nuns of his Congregation gathered around his bedside. He was given the last Sacraments and everyone thought that he was about to die. Everyone, that is, except Don Orione himself. Once he had got over the first effects of the stroke he knew that he would live. He still had work to do.

He was the despair of those charged with the job of looking after him. One of his priests, Fr Costanzo Costamagna, was serving as infirmarian. He was the man whom Don Orione had called ten years before from his market stall to be a priest.

Fr Costamagna told me of the difficulty with which he had to contend at that period. His superiors, the nurses, the nuns and the doctor had all told him that Don Orione must at all costs rest and remain relaxed. His job above all else, they said, was to protect Don Orione from himself and to contrive by one means or another to make him follow the doctor's orders. Strict rest must be observed, "and you must make him observe it".

But even before he could attempt to put this into practice, Don Orione was busy conspiring with him: "I must start working. Get me a pen and paper at once. I rely upon you not to let me down. You must shield me from these people." Obediently he would do as Don Orione asked and, instead of being the doctor's watchdog, he would spend his time standing guard at the door, ready to give warning of the doctor's approach. When he signalled that 'the enemy' was coming, Don Orione would shoot back into bed. Then, when the nurse, sister or doctor arrived, he would smile sweetly at them from between the sheets.

The Sisters thought that he should be tempted to eat. They asked him what he would like for a meal. "I am 65 years of age and I have never thought about what I should eat," he told them. "I take whatever is necessary to stoke the fire and maintain my energy." He joked and quipped with everyone as usual. When he began to recover, the doctor was surprised that he had maintained his weight so well. "You should not be surprised," he told them. "I still have my sins and they are heavy."

Outside the hospital, men and women who had learned of his illness from the radio and the press were queuing from morning till night. They came all day anxiously enquiring about him, believing that he was at death's door. Inside, with his angel-guardian still keeping watch for him, Don Orione sat on his bed writing Easter greetings to scores of his priests and friends.

Don Orione was right and the pessimists proved wrong. He recovered. Messages of congratulation poured in from all over Italy. It is clear that, whilst he thanked God for his recovery, he realised that he had little time to spare. Before long he was back on the job, working, if possible, harder than ever.

He resumed his weekly visits to Milan and Genoa, sitting all day as before receiving people of every type. Once as he travelled back to Tortona he told a companion: "I am utterly weary. But I know that God has given me the word that consoles and I must do this." Another night, as he laboriously climbed the inconvenient steps leading to the Central Station at Milan he stopped at every two or three steps to get his breath. When he finally got to the top, he said: "My heart is like a cord. One day it is going to snap." But still he rose at 4.30 each morning and was in the chapel before anyone else.

As unobtrusively as they could, the members of his Order tried to safeguard his health. He now always had a travelling companion and in the end an excuse was found for the infirmarian, his 'guardian angel', to sleep in his room.

One evening that autumn a homeless boy was brought to see him. Don Orione gave the boy his bed until another was found for him. He fixed up for himself two boards propped up on a pile of books.

The small room itself was as simple as it could be, combining both bedroom and study. It remains today as it was then. It has a stone floor, an iron bedstead, a simple writing desk, a small library of devotional books, mainly lives of saints, and a well-used copy of Dante's *Divine Comedy*. There is a rusty old iron stove, two rather tasteless statues of the 'popular' Italian type, one of the Madonna, the other of the Sacred Heart. In one sense his room reflects how, apart from his beloved Dante, he had turned his back upon all his cultural interests. He wanted his devotion to be 'of the people'.

A very realistic crucifix of the sort beloved by Italians hangs on the wall along with a few sacred pictures. There is one of Don Bosco sitting in state in his chair after death, recalling how the young Luigi was one of those who formed the guard of honour around that chair at the time. Beside the bed hangs the large Polish flag.

On the writing table is a skull which he always kept there. Written across the forehead in Don Orione's own hand are the words "Ti annunzio l'amore di Gesù"—"I tell you the love of Jesus". Its origin is unknown, but examination reveals a long joint running across the back. It is the skull of someone who had been operated upon for madness. Whether Don Orione was aware of this no one knows. It seems likely that he may have been, for he had a great love and pity for the mentally sick, and the asylums which he and his Congregation started are to be found in every part of Italy, in Switzerland, in South America and elsewhere.

*

In 1955 at the opening of a new chest clinic in Milan by the Minister of Labour, I met the architect, Sig. Gazolo, who told me a story from this period which seems to call for no comment of mine.

In December 1939, Don Orione had been asked to speak to some 300 friends of his work in the city. When he arrived he was clearly under great physical strain. He climbed on to the platform, the chairman announced that he would speak, and as he was about to rise he turned suddenly to Gazolo who sat at his side.

"I can't do it," he said, "I'm too tired. You must do me a favour."

"Willingly, if I can," the other whispered back.

"You must talk to them."

"But I can't. I have never spoken in public."

"Do it, *please*. You will be all right."

The whole whispered conversation was over in a minute and before Gazolo had had time to collect his thoughts or to form the slightest idea what he was going to say, he was on his feet in front of an influential audience. He took a glance at Don Orione and saw that he was fixing his eyes intently upon him, as though he was willing something very strongly. Gazolo spoke for 45 minutes, without notes, with no preparation and in a style quite unlike his own. "I just felt that I was like a loud-speaker for Don Orione," he told me.

Three years later he read an article in a paper by the poet Medici who had sat on that same platform that day. Medici described the event, gave a full account of Gazolo's speech and expressed his opinion that it was not Gazolo who spoke but "some mysterious power emanating from Don Orione". "I felt that I could have done the same," he wrote.

*

On Christmas Eve, Don Orione called his young secretary to him: "Now you must go home for Christmas and keep your mother company," he said. "I shall be all right on my own."

He handed him two tins of biscuits. One he was to give to his mother as a present. The other he was to take on December 26 to a young priest who had had tuberculosis and had been given a lonely little church and presbytery where he lived alone miles up in the mountains. He did not belong to the Sons of Divine Providence but Don Orione had somehow come to hear of his case.

"Give him these," he said, "to let him know that he is not forgotten."

The seminarian took them, as requested. He found the young priest absolutely alone. Don Orione's gift was the only one he received that Christmas. But it was one he would never forget.

*

On Christmas Day his followers began to think that he was perhaps on the way to a full recovery, for he succeeded in celebrating the three Christmas Masses. But his faithful infirmarian and the seminarian who acted as his secretary both knew that often, all through that month, Don Orione had spent hours sitting propped up in bed at night suffering from palpitations of the heart and feelings of suffocation. In the morning he would get up and say his Mass as though his rest had been undisturbed. He said it with a hot water bottle at his back.

"Don't tell anyone," he would say of his broken nights. "We must get our work done as usual."

This situation continued through January 1940, and the early part of February.

For years he had written daily a brief 'thought for the day' to be displayed in the Tortona mother house. He even maintained the practice while he was in South America, sending back a brief message every day. Collectively they reveal his mind and simple piety, his hopes and fears, more vividly than could any carefully written work.

One day, early in February 1940, the daily thought which he put on the notice board was "To die standing". On January 17, he had approved the drawings of the enormous "Cottolengo" which was to be built in Milan and which would provide help and shelter for almost every sort of unfortunate. After the long fight of past years it gave him particular joy when Cardinal Schuster approved it in the most generous terms.

"It is customary for God to build his own houses," he wrote. "I cannot but bless this project."

On February 6, he went to Milan for the last time. Suddenly, when he was at the station he said: "I must go and pay my respects to the Cardinal." This was unusual, for he was usually meticulously careful to go, like any ordinary priest, only by appointment. As he slowly climbed the steps of the house in which lived the Cardinal who had so vigorously opposed him in the past, he said: "Cardinal Schuster has really been very kind to us. I want to go and say 'thank you' to him for all that he has done for us."

The Cardinal later said that Don Orione had told him that day: "Your Eminence should be very careful. In this moment all Italy looks to you. The country is going to rely upon you and you can play an important part." Four months later Italy went to war. The Cardinal did, as Don Orione had urged, play an important part, with his attitude to Fascism very much modified. It was as though Don Orione, at death's door, felt compelled to take his last farewell of the Cardinal and advise him in this way.

Two days later he went to both Turin and Genoa, making it an even fuller and busier day than usual. At five o'clock next morning he had another heart attack. He asked for and received the last Sacraments. For hours he hung between life and death. Later that same day, February 9, he had a return attack.

Again everyone was convinced that he was about to die. He spoke only with difficulty. Even so he managed to tell his young amateur secretary that he needed all his writing equipment. The seminarian was astonished and appalled. Don Orione insisted.

"Go up to the infirmary. There you will find a small bed-table. Put it here so that I can write."

The seminarian went instead to Don Sterpi, Don Orione's faithful right-hand man and successor. Don Sterpi told him to beg Don Orione not to work. "He is very seriously ill and he must rest," he said.

It was to no purpose. Calmly but very purposefully, rallying his strength for the effort, Don Orione said: "You must tell Don Sterpi that I would like to carry on with my duty up to death and I willingly renounce my life."

The table was fetched and set up by the bed of the desperately sick man. He took his pen and began to write. All his life he had carried on a vigorous apostolate of the pen. But when just three words were on the paper the pen fell from his hand. He tried again without success. His will was still strong but his body was not.

Don Orione looked resigned. "All right, if I can't write I'll dictate," he whispered. He was attempting as always to keep contact with his priests abroad. This was to be a letter to one of his beloved South Americans. He began it with the words: "I write with one foot in the grave . . ." He knew that this attack was the last he would survive.

Each day he dictated a page or two of that letter. He was determined to finish it. By the evening of the fourth day it had grown to eight pages.

"Do you mind if I call you very early tomorrow morning?" he asked his secretary. "I want to finish it."

At 5 a.m. with the young man again at his bedside, he huskily dictated the concluding passages. The letter was finished.

He had wished "to die standing", in action, and it was not going to be his fault if he did not.

*

The crisis passed to the extent that he was able to get up and with difficulty say his Mass. Meanwhile his doctor and Don Sterpi were trying to persuade him to go from Tortona to stay at a house which the Congregation had at San Remo, on the Italian Riviera. At last he agreed.

"The doctor has said that I must go and so I suppose I should," he told his secretary.

But the arrangement clearly did not appeal to him. For many years, whenever he was in Tortona, he had made a practice of giving the seminarians a 'good-night talk'. Weak as he was, he gave them a particularly long one that night. In it he made it perfectly obvious that he knew that he was going away to die.

A few days earlier he had called together a little group of those closest to him, Don Sterpi, his doctor, the infirmarian, his seminarian-secretary and one or two old priests. "I am only going away," he told them, "because you want me to go. But I tell you that I shall not come back alive. When I return it will be in my coffin."

Most of the others protested, refusing to believe that the end would come so soon. He had recovered so many times, why not again? But Don Sterpi who had been near to him for years did not share their optimism. He called them together and told them that he would accept no responsibility for the move to San Remo.

"I believe him," he said sadly, "when he says that he will not come back alive."

When Don Orione left for the warmer climate of the Italian Riviera on March 9, he deliberately avoided Don Sterpi. He knew that the parting would be difficult for him and so spared him it altogether.

He and the 20-year-old seminarian-secretary travelled to San Remo by train, Don Orione insisting that they should go third class as usual. On the way a railwayman came into the packed compartment. "This is Don Orione, isn't it?" he said. "I'll find a better seat for you."

The secretary went with him and soon came and fetched Don Orione. When he saw that the seat they had found for him was in a first-class carriage he cried: "No, No. No cushions for me, that is too much altogether," and went back to his original place.

As he walked his back was bent and he dragged his feet. But all the way he joked with his companion and with the other people in the compartment whenever he was not busying himself with writing the inevitable letters. When the secretary showed him a bottle of oxygen which the doctor had given him for use in case of emergency, Don Orione laughed it to scorn.

For some reason the message that he was on the way had not yet reached the house in San Remo and so when they got there they found that all the Sisters but one had gone on a pilgrimage to a local shrine. No meal was prepared and nothing had been done for his reception. Don Orione went into the chapel to pray, then walked round behind the altar. There on a wall he found hanging a picture of himself. "Take it down, take it down," he exclaimed. "We don't want my picture hanging in church."

It was late when the nuns returned home. They at once began to apologise but Don Orione told them they had no need to worry. He went off to bed—only to discover that there was no light other than a tiny votive lamp which burned in a glass in front of a picture of the Madonna.

"Don't you think," Don Orione asked the infirmarian with a chuckle, "that this place is exactly like a mortuary chapel?"

He enjoyed the joke far better than his companion did.

Next day a specialist arrived. His patient clearly saw no purpose in his professional ministrations. "I am going to die, so why go to all this bother and expense?" seemed to be his attitude, but he accepted it now with resignation. Once he would have rebelled. The specialist, misled by his constant banter, gave it as his opinion that far from dying he would yet live to a ripe old age. But Don Orione, who learned of this, merely shook his head and said: "Poor man, he doesn't know a thing."

Next morning, and for the next three days, Don Orione got down to work early. He said his Mass, attended all the devotions of the house, refused any special diet, and when he was not saying the Rosary, wrote for hours on end. His secretary tried to persuade him to go down to the sea but Don Orione told him to go and enjoy himself, he was too busy to come.

At last, one afternoon the infirmarian managed to get him to go for a rest in his room. The stratagem he employed was to persuade him to let one of the Sisters repair his one and only ragged cassock. Later on, still feeling pleased with himself for having at last achieved so much, he tiptoed into Don Orione's room. He found him sitting writing, surrounded by a pile of letters. When he later took them to be mailed he counted them. There were 22. To a protest that he was working too hard Don Orione cheerfully replied: "It's all right. We'll have a long rest in Paradise."

*

Don Orione was sitting up in bed trying to pare the corns from his knees with a knife when the infirmarian entered his room one day. "I don't know what is going to happen to this old body," he told him, "but I want to get rid of these things before I die. We don't want a lot of people to see them and start making something out of it."

The corns had come from much time spent in prayer.

*

On March 12 he got up at his usual early hour, again said his Mass, and then wanted to serve Mass for another priest but was with difficulty persuaded to let the infirmarian do it instead.

Again he wrote letters nearly all day. He stopped once to ask for Dante's *Divine Comedy* and Manzoni's *Promessi Sposi* (The Beloved).

"I want some exact quotations," he said. "These are important letters and I must get them right."

Remembering that it was the anniversary of the coronation of Pius XII he sent the Holy Father a telegram of congratulations. At 4 o'clock in the afternoon he received some old friends from Tortona. He ate his supper, received another visitor, wrote more letters, this time standing, because of the difficulty he found in breathing. He read a life of St Francis of Assisi for a while.

At 10 o'clock he considerately sent the infirmarian off to bed, telling him that he must surely be tired. Then he settled down for the night. But within a few minutes he was calling the infirmarian back again.

He had had his third and last stroke. The infirmarian gave him an injection, and then a blast of oxygen. When the priests and nuns in the house all came advising that a doctor should be called, he told them not to bother, he wanted no fuss made.

He looked serenely at the infirmarian for a moment, said "I'm going", then "Gesù, Gesù, Gesù," and quietly sank down like a man going to sleep.

As the news spread of the death of Don Orione, Friend of the Poor, a great crowd of people from every walk of life began to arrive to see the man whom each had felt to be his special friend. The Pope, the Queen of Italy, Cardinals, all sent messages of condolence. But above all it was the poor for whom he had had such a special love who thronged the streets as the cortège a few days later made its way through one town after another.

The body was taken from San Remo through Genoa and Milan, where he had had some of his hardest fights and biggest successes, through

Voghera, where he had gone to the Franciscans as a boy, through Pontecurone, where he was born and people were already venerating him as their local saint, and through a dozen other towns, to Tortona.

At every village, town and city the populace turned out to line the route. The streets of Pontecurone were covered with violets picked by the peasants and strewn over the cobbles.

The son of Vittorio Orione the *sulli* had come home in triumph. Even poorer, if possible, than when he left his home village, but loved and respected by millions.

CHAPTER X

Still at Work

WHEN I went to Italy to gather material for a biography of Don Orione I did so because I was attracted by what I knew of his works of charity and mercy.

I was also interested in an idea. It is one which I discuss in my next chapter. Briefly it is this: In the modern State in general and the Welfare State in particular, in which the search for social justice has so largely replaced the practice of Christian charity, what role, if any, is there for the works of Congregations such as that founded by Don Orione?

Thus it was an idea as much as a person which set me off travelling the length and breadth of Italy in the steps of Luigi Orione.

But it was not long before that person had captivated me. He was so much bigger than the man I had set out to find. He was so much more human and still so much a saint for our time.

There was, I discovered, something extraordinarily fascinating about his personality. I had not been in Italy long before I began to feel the attraction of that personality, to an almost uncanny extent, not as something belonging to the past but as a living, potent force. I felt that I was both working *for* him and *with* him.

I asked thousands of questions about him and obtained, by means of cross-examination, the independent testimony of hundreds of the most diverse types of people from princes of the Church to the simplest peasants.

The gestures and expressions of the people I interviewed fascinated me, for often, as they talked of him, these were as revealing as the words they spoke. I saw Don Orione's characteristic gestures and expressions reflected, mirror-like, in theirs. Over and over again when I mentioned his name, eyes would suddenly light up at the recollection of some particular incident, or maybe some mere glance of his.

When people recalled conversations they had had with him or told anecdotes from their own experience, their arms would wave in the air as they tried to convey by wild gesticulation something of the enormous vitality and spirit of the man, or to imitate his own gestures. As likely as not the gestures would suddenly stop, and the eyes cease to blaze, as they attempted instead to copy one of his expressions of enormous benevolence or to convey something of a mood or some act of infinite tenderness.

I watched these sharp changes fascinated, for often it seemed that they could not be talking of the same man. It was almost as though they were miming a dialogue between two opposite—extremely opposite—types. Nothing else could have described so vividly for me the dynamic character of the little priest from Tortona and the enormous charity to which his dynamism was so providentially harnessed.

I had spent the morning of one day in leisurely sightseeing in Venice and had enjoyed to the full the loveliness of the canals with their bridges, as I travelled them by water-bus. Later, still under their spell, I sat bewailing the modern craze for speed and extolling the sanity of a city which in this day and generation uses slow-moving water-traffic instead of high-powered automobiles.

Then the telephone rang and I found myself talking to the secretary of the Cardinal-Patriarch of Venice. He told me that the Cardinal would like to meet me. If I could be at his residence in just 30 minutes' time he would wedge a brief quarter of an hour's chat between two other engagements.

The leisurely speed of the motor launch as it made its way between the gondolas on the crowded Grand Canal seemed less attractive as the minutes sped by. With just a few moments to spare I hurried across St Mark's Square, past the Gothic splendour of the Doge's Palace and the great Byzantine Cathedral and up the steps of the adjoining palace.

"You have come to learn about Don Orione," the Cardinal Patriarch said as he greeted me.

"I have," I replied. "But I would like you to tell me at once, without stopping to think over your words, what you believe to have been his outstanding quality."

There was not a moment's hesitation.

"Don Orione was the most charitable man I ever knew. His charity went further than that of anyone of whom I ever read or heard. It went beyond all the normal limits. He believed you could conquer the world by love."

The response which the name of Don Orione still evokes in the most unlikely quarters was illustrated for me in a thoroughly Italian fashion one Sunday morning. I had left Tortona by car for Genoa, a journey which would take me along the edge of the Italian Riviera. But first I wanted to trace a man who could, I had been told, confirm a certain story for me. He lived in a remote rural area where roads were bad and houses few and far between. When at length we came to the district in which he lived we had great difficulty in finding his address and, having arrived at last, we found that he was not at home.

Perhaps, said his neighbours, he might be

having lunch at an inn which he frequented. The local Communist Party was meeting in the inn parlour when we got there. We broke in on its deliberations and that perhaps partly explains why the answers we got from the Party members were brief and to the point. But they conveyed to us, in as few words as possible, the fact that he was not eating his lunch there that day. The comrades were clearly anxious to continue with their discussions and had no time to spare for us.

Then we mentioned that we particularly wanted to run our man to earth because we understood that he had a good first-hand story about Don Orione, for whose biography I was gathering material.

At the mere mention of Don Orione's name the Communists' attitude changed at once.

Our man, they said co-operatively, might possibly have gone to see some relatives who lived some ten miles away. They tried to tell us how to get to them but this place seemed even more inaccessible, judging by their complicated directions, than the last.

"As it is for Don Orione, we will take you there ourselves," said their spokesman who, no doubt, was as good an atheistic Communist as Giovanni Guareschi's Mayor Peppone himself.

The comrades each seized a motor cycle or auto-scooter from against the wall and, with half a dozen outriders fore and another half dozen aft, we tore through the Italian countryside. Only when they had seen us safely to our destination did they leave us for the long ride back to resume their Communist Party branch meeting. Tortona itself is adjacent to the Po valley and this was the genuine Don Camillo country in more senses than one.

*

Wherever he went Don Orione exercised a quite exceptional influence upon others. Many a man left all he had to follow the Christ he saw reflected in Don Orione's life. The houses of the Sons of Divine Providence and of Don Orione's female Congregations are full of people who responded to his call. More often than not the call was not to do anything spectacular or glamorous. Rather it was just the reverse. There are attractive girls who heard it and left all to go and tend senile women, cantankerous, incontinent old men, or the hopelessly and incurably insane for the rest of their days. Talk to them, or cross-examine them as I have done, and you will find that for them such work has come to mean everything. They could wish for nothing more satisfying or rewarding. Their response to the call to go to the limits—and beyond the limits—of ordinary Christian charity has brought them greater happiness than they could ever have imagined was possible.

Take, for example, the case of Fr Nicco, whom I saw at work in Genoa, and the layman who was his close associate.

In the warm darkness of a June night I sat watching a slap-stick film, shown in the open air. The cinematograph machine had been set up on a low roof which was surrounded on all four sides by the tall blocks of a mental hospital for women.

Nearby sat, hunched up, a woman who said nothing but "Good morning, Good morning," all day long and who now turned from time to time to say it to me. Row upon row of women with strange faces, and many of them with strangely shaped heads—some much too large, others too small—sat facing the screen. They were, in their own way, an unusually happy audience. They greeted comic and serious parts of the film alike with a mixture of giggles, excited shouts of mirth or strange exultant animal noises, according to the character and seriousness of their mental disorder.

High up on the top floor of each block were the barred windows of rooms in which the worst cases had to be confined. And against the bars, making an already somewhat macabre scene still more macabre, were pressed the faces of women who, with wild eyes, tried to see something of what was going on below.

My companions were the Rector, Fr Nicco, and a 70-year-old professor. For more than 20 years the professor, one of Italy's foremost specialists in the treatment and cure of mental diseases, has given half of every day free of charge to the hospital.

"I met Don Orione in December 1933," the professor told me. "He asked for my help and that was sufficient. I have loved every minute I have put in here. My happiest hours are spent in this place."

The institution, a teaching hospital famous for its cures, is the equal of any, anywhere. One piece of its expensive surgical equipment was given some years ago by the man who was at that time Genoa's Communist mayor. The hospital houses 150 mentally deficient orphan girls, 100 epileptic women, 250 mad women and 150 mentally deficient children of from 2 to 14 years of age.

We left the strange audience still watching their Sunday night cinema show and went through a darkened wing of the building together. As we walked down one of its corridors, I was conscious of something or someone sliding quietly past me, then shuffling off into the darkness. Fr Nicco slipped away and a few minutes later came back holding a bent little woman who carried a small bundle of rags over her shoulder. She had wandered from her room on the top floor whilst the film show was on.

"She takes that little bundle everywhere with her," the Rector told me. "She is deaf and she howls in an enormously loud and uncontrolled voice from morning till night."

But now, happy to be in his company, she was quiet. Grinning, she trustingly put her hand in his as he took her upstairs again with no fuss or force whatsoever.

Fr Nicco, incidentally, was one of the 'bright boys' of his Congregation and so was sent to study at the great Gregorian University in Rome. He dreamed of going to the missions but instead Don Orione asked him to become Rector of the Community which administered this hospital for mentally disordered women and girls. I could not help wondering how he had reacted to the request.

"Weren't you disappointed—and appalled—at the work he had chosen for you?" I asked him.

"Yes, at first," Fr Nicco replied. "But Don Orione asked me to do it and that was sufficient. Now I love the work, as he knew I would."

The example of Don Orione himself, and that of his priests and nuns, has inspired many laymen, like the professor in Genoa, to give their time and skill to the poorest and the most needy.

After an afternoon among the ruins of Pompeii, I was travelling back to Naples where I was to make a visit to a hospital. When the car broke down, I hailed a passing motorist who willingly took me to my destination in the city. The delay had not worried me unduly, since so far as I knew, no preparations had been made for my arrival and so no inconvenience had been caused to anyone but myself.

When, however, I arrived at the hospital, a former palace given by a Countess, sister-in-law of Emmanuel III, to the followers of Don Orione, I found 27 doctors waiting for me. All were from Naples. Working on a rota, they between them staffed the hospital free of charge. They also, at their own expense, kept it supplied with drugs and dressings and had begged from their friends the money with which to buy the most modern equipment possible.

The hospital was the only one in the city where every form of treatment could be obtained free of charge. I was shown around the building by an 18-year-old youth. He was a war victim who had lost both legs but now walked up and down the stairs with hardly a hint of the fact that his limbs were artificial. The doctors followed with enormous pride. He was one of their big successes.

"Why," I asked one of them, "do you give so much of your time to this work when you are already busy in your private practices?"

"We are all under the spell of Don Orione," he replied. "We give some of our time. He gave himself completely."

*

Going about Italy one felt that Don Orione was still alive. Everyone who had known him spoke of him as if he was even now amongst them.

Archbishop Montini, the former Vatican Pro-Secretary of State who is now exerting such an enormous influence in Milan, is a case in point. When I told him the purpose of my visit, he said quite naturally: "So you are a guest of Don Orione. You are in good hands. He will look after you." No one overhearing the conversation would have guessed that Don Orione had been dead for 15 years.

Not the least of Don Orione's striking characteristics was his uncanny (or, rather, providential) ability to get the things he needed most. This characteristic was so well known that it earned him the title of "God's bandit".

It was shown, for example, on that famous occasion when he got, unexpectedly and almost inexplicably, the exact sum of money required for his first boys' school in Tortona whilst he was still a 20-year-old seminarian. And throughout his life such occurrences were almost normal. Most of his houses, and those since acquired by his Congregation, came by some such means.

Genoa is ringed by fort-topped hills. On one of these, Camaldoli, Don Orione had a small house and a little bit of land. Immediately above the house and running right up to the top of the hill was a village composed of a number of villas and a large house, or rather, a former nobleman's palace, and a church.

In the palace lived an actor, Daniel Chiarella, who acquired bit by bit the whole of the village and the land that went with it. He used the villas for the purpose of accommodating his many actor friends and gradually built up a somewhat Bohemian community there. As time went on he acquired more and more land until he came right down to, and surrounded, the little bit which was owned by Don Orione's Congregation.

One day Chiarella went to Don Orione and tried to persuade him to sell the house and land. When Don Orione refused he became very angry and swore that by one means or another he would get it. Calmly, Don Orione told him that on the contrary, far from his incorporating the Congregation's house and land into his village, it was the Congregation which would in time swallow up all his property.

For years Chiarella lived in grandeur in the palace on the top of the hill but in 1939 it became clear that he had overreached himself. Desperately, he began to sell his land and property again but by the following year he was bankrupt. Every bit of his land and property went. It was offered for sale at the price of one million *lire*. By now Don Orione was dead but Don Sterpi was able to step in and buy it all with money given him for the purpose by a nobleman who admired the Congregation's work.

Today the palace, every one of the villas, the entire village, including a dilapidated church which Chiarella had desecrated, together comprise a colony for misfits and unfortunates of every type. It is known as the "Villaggio della carità Don Luigi Orione". In one house are boys with a contagious eye disease; another is the home of a number of badly deformed men and youths; yet another houses homeless old men. Other houses are used as hospitals, convalescent homes, sanatoria. One group is used as a colony for mental defectives. The palace itself is a home for sick, impoverished and senile priests.

Equally in line with the Don Orione tradition is the way in which the Sons of Divine Providence acquired the largest of all their premises.

Not long before World War II Mussolini began to build an enormous Fascist youth headquarters on a hill on the outskirts of Rome. Crowning one of the buildings was a great plinth which was to carry a huge statue of Mussolini. It would look out over all Rome and, when it was illuminated at night, all Rome would see it.

The buildings, which were still not completed when the war began, are now in the hands of the Sons of Divine Providence who use them as a great home and training centre for hundreds of war-mutilated boys. An adjoining building, almost as large as the other, is used by them as a technical college for orphans. No statue of Mussolini ever took its place on the great plinth. Instead a very lovely statue of the Madonna—one of the largest in the world—stands there with arms outstretched as though to take all humanity to her breast.

How did it happen?

When the Nazis were evacuating Rome they put a number of troops into the great, almost-completed Fascist youth headquarters on the edge of the city to cover their retreat. By the time the troops left, the Allies were in Rome. In the fighting, large numbers of civilians lost their lives, families were broken up, and hungry orphans and homeless children wandered the streets. These children hunted for food by day and slept where they could by night. Often they formed themselves into gangs for their own protection and in order to loot and forage for food more effectively.

It was in these conditions of chaos that one gang of desperate boys, led by some men of criminal tendencies, established themselves in a part of the great Fascist youth headquarters. The foremost of their leaders, to disarm suspicion, disguised himself as a priest and called the gang "The Crusaders for Good".

The ruse worked. When the Allies took over Rome they inspected all the buildings formerly occupied by the Fascists and requisitioned them for their own purposes. But when they reached this particular building on Monte Mario they found the so-called priest and his "Crusaders for Good" already established in one corner of it. They decided that since it was apparently being used for good purposes it should not be touched.

Before long the gang had become so audacious in its thieving raids on army supplies that the order was given to shoot its members on sight. Even so, they do not seem to have been identified for some time as the "Crusaders for Good". Gradually the building, and the great neighbouring one, filled up with allied troops and installations. The British established themselves in one end of the building in which the gang still lived, and installed a radio transmitter there. The French took over a series of smaller buildings associated with it and which are today workshops for the orphans and *mutilatini*. American soldiers occupied part of the other big building, while the Italian forces who accompanied them had the rest. Mixing with these troops of various nations was the gang of street boys by now completely wild and uncontrolled.

When order was restored in the city, the police began to realise that this was a gang of thieves, although they still thought that its leader was a genuine priest trying without success to control the boys he had befriended. For that reason they treated him with respect. None the less, they got in touch with the ecclesiastical authorities suggesting that they should take a hand in regularising the situation and that it should be dealt with as an urgent matter.

The Vicar General of Rome decided that this was a job for the Sons of Divine Providence. He called for Fr Piccinini of the Congregation's General Council. To him he explained his doubts about the 'priest'. He urged Fr Piccinini to try by some means or other to gain control of the 70 boys.

"We can't send them back on the streets," he said. "This is just the sort of thing Don Orione would have loved to do. Take care of them if you can."

The job of winning the confidence of the boys and wooing them away from their leader called for almost as much tact as Don Orione himself had had to use years before when he was dealing with the situation created by the Messina earthquake. So, too, did the delicate job of gaining permission for them to stay where they were—for the military authorities of half a dozen different nations were involved.

In the end all the necessary authorisations were obtained, the 'priest' was unmasked as an impostor, arrested, charged with false pretences and jailed. Even so, some of the other men who had been in the leadership of the gang took every sheet, blanket, pot and pan in the place when they pulled out together one night.

Slowly priests of the Sons of Divine Providence began to move in and the boys settled down. Problems followed each other thick and fast. New political parties were springing up and all were looking for premises. One after another they tried to lay claim, before the Allies left, to the big buildings on Monte Mario. In particular, the Communists were persistently trying to persuade the Americans to let them have their part of the former Fascist youth headquarters.

At this point, Winston Churchill who was in Rome, went to the block where the British had their radio transmitter in order to make a broadcast. Whilst he was there he saw some of the boys—who now numbered some 150—and at once took an interest in them. When one of the Sons of Divine Providence one day got a message that he should report to the British military authorities, he thought that after all their trouble they were now going to have their premises taken from them. He went into the presence of a top-ranking British general, fervently muttering *Aves* to himself.

But the greeting he got was a friendly one. "Our Prime Minister has been enquiring about the work you are doing," he was told. "How can we help you?"

The priest had expected to have to fight to keep the building. Instead he had suddenly to think, not of losing all, but of having, it seemed, whatever practicable things he cared to ask for. "If we could have some sheets it would help," he said diffidently. "All ours were stolen." A soldier noted his request and looked up in expectation of the next one. Gaining courage as he went along, the priest added: "We need blankets too." This item was also noted, and still it was clear that the British general expected more demands to be made upon him. Then the priest let himself go. He asked for mobile sanitary services, beds, "perhaps a jeep or two" and anything else he thought he could use. The officer said he would come at eleven o'clock next morning to tell him which of the items he could supply.

Prompt on the minute next day he arrived at Monte Mario. The priest showed him the bare-walled buildings which by now lacked even the most elementary interior fittings. "If you make this place fit to live in," he told the General, "we can collect another hundred boys off the streets at once and save them from becoming criminals."

On the following day a British captain arrived with a team of workers whose number soon grew to more than forty. They put cellophane into the empty windows and did first-aid repairs to the interior. They even built a bakery. By the time they left, a month later, the whole of the buildings had not only been restored—they had been formally handed over by the General to the Sons of Divine Providence. From then on their possession of the building was guaranteed by the Allied authorities themselves.

Another 20 homeless boys were soon housed there. Then someone suggested that something should be done about Rome's many war-mutilated children. The Sons of Divine Providence went out and soon brought back to Monte Mario a first batch of sixty.

Gradually the work grew until the whole of the one building was filled with hundreds of orphans, the other with still more hundreds of war-mutilated children. Some of the boys were without hands, some lacked feet or legs. All were given a home and trained to fit themselves, despite their handicaps, for life.

Today the workshops in which the *mutilatini* do engineering, pottery, woodwork, commercial art and a host of other crafts are famous throughout Italy.

And at night the illuminated Madonna of Monte Mario looks out over the Eternal City and all Rome knows that beside her stands one of Italy's greatest and most famous works of mercy, run by the followers of Don Luigi Orione.

CHAPTER XI

Charity or Justice?

THE work started by Don Orione and continued by his followers excites the admiration of all who come in contact with it. Its humanity and the sheer determination of these good men and women to seek out all those whom the world rejects or forgets never fail to evoke a generous response.

It is all very Christian, very impressive, very moving. But is it necessary in the modern world? Does not charity of this type really belong to the Middle Ages when everything depended upon the private benefactor and nothing upon the State? Or to the period of the industrial revolution when wealth-crazy industrialists trampled the poor in the dust and then salved their own consciences—and prevented revolution—by supporting organisations which toned down the worst effects of their greed?

In the Socialist and Communist movements and in some liberal circles, too, there are people who believe that by supporting charitable causes one is actually doing the poor and the unfortunate a disservice, for the State is thereby enabled to escape its clear responsibility for those whose welfare should be its concern. Social justice, they say, demands that the mentally or physically handicapped should be the care of the community as a whole, in other words, of the State. In a just and decent society there would be no poverty. Justice demands that all men should receive an adequate income, be given decent conditions and, ideally, be assured security from the cradle to the grave.

The fight for social justice has undoubtedly helped towards the ending of many grave abuses. Life for the working class is better today because men with sensitive social consciences have been willing to speak out and, if need be, to fight for better conditions.

The logical end to that search for social justice, which has been a major preoccupation now for half a century, would appear to be the Welfare State. And the Welfare State would appear to leave little room or necessity for Christian charity. In such a State certain minimum standards are guaranteed to all alike, regardless of what contribution they may or may not be able to make to society. When they are sick, they can go to an efficient, well organised and amply financed hospital. Should they be badly handicapped in some way—physically deformed or mentally deficient—the State takes care of them, providing them with food, shelter, and expert professional attention.

Yet, in practice, it is not all plain sailing. The replacement of charity by justice tends to lead to a decline in the sense of vocation. It is not unusual today, for example, for the most modern of hospitals and sanatoria because of a shortage of staff to be accommodating fewer people than they might hold despite all those who need their services.

Who of us would nurse the hopelessly, violently insane or the disgustingly senile if we could earn the same money doing some more congenial work—unless we had a strong sense of vocation? Where that sense of vocation is absent, such occupations, from being ones which attracted the best, may become ones which attract only types who could do nothing else—people for whom their work is just a routine job.

Experience, moreover, has shown that there tends to be something missing from the big State, or purely commercial, hospital, despite all its efficiency. In the less well financed voluntary hospital there is an intangible something which the others lack. It is intangible, but it is enormously valuable and important to the individual because it is based upon respect for him as a person, as anyone who has experienced treatment in establishments of both kinds can confirm. That something is Christian charity.

And experience has shown, too, that there tend to be curious gaps in the Welfare State. The State, after all, is primarily interested in today's and tomorrow's citizens, rather than yesterday's. This presumably explains why it is that old people more than anyone today tend as a class to suffer real privation. The whole trend is towards the loss of any real sense of responsibility for them on anyone's part.

You may see them in the winter sitting all day long in the reading rooms of public libraries, making the most of the free heat and relative comfort there. Then they go 'home' to lonely rooms with empty grates and half-empty pantries.

It is not enough to provide such people with larger pensions and special housing facilities—although these are, in present circumstances, urgently needed. They need affection, a sense of 'belonging', of still being wanted on this earth.

When Fr Paul Bidone of the Sons of Divine Providence arrived in England in 1949, with a ten-shilling note, his only wealth, clasped in his hand, intent on extending the work of Don Orione to the United Kingdom, the Welfare State, backed by all political parties, was in its first heady, self-confident stages. All the talk was of State-provided security "from the cradle to the grave". The moment might have appeared to any observer as a peculiarly inopportune one in which to come with plans for 'old-fashioned' works of mercy and of charity. But instinctively, just as Don Orione would have done, Fr Bidone did the right thing. He started a home for old people. In so doing he met a real human need. Today State officials and welfare organisations besiege him with requests to expand his work. Old people implore him to give them a home where they will be made to feel of some worth as individuals. Over and over again they tell him: "Nowadays old folk like us are not wanted at any price."

So, too, is it in the United States where the Welfare State does not, as such, exist but where the weak and the poor can still, in a fiercely competitive society, go to the wall unseen and unregarded. There also, in Boston, among the Italian émigré population, the first work of the Congregation has been among the old.

Nor is the need confined to the old alone. Even in the best organised of Welfare States, or in the wealthiest of competitive societies, whole large groups such as the chronic, incurably sick, the mentally deficient children, epileptics and others, tend to find themselves unwanted and even resented. The same is true of the social misfits of the sort which the Sons of Divine Providence also make their special care in so many of their "little Cottolengos".

To say that if everyone practised social justice Christian charity would not be needed is to leave human nature out of account. For that matter one may just as easily turn it round the other way and say that if everyone practised Christian charity the fight for social justice would be unnecessary. Both are needed. The work and example of the followers of Don Orione are needed today perhaps more than ever. For they are keeping alive a principle as well as meeting a human need.

Yet in a world in which materialism, greed and selfishness flourish among both rich and poor, it is not enough to have small islands of Christian charity and to think that the example and influence of these alone will bring about a revolution in society.

The great "Cottolengo", that city within a city in Turin stands as a living proof of this. Nowhere on earth will you find more selfless men and women dedicated to works of mercy among the scorned and rejected. It stands there, in the very heart of industrial Turin, and has stood for a century and a half, as a glorious example of Christian charity in practice. If charity alone were enough, then Turin ought to be the most Christian city on earth; social justice ought to reign supreme and discontent be unknown there. Instead, Turin is better known today for its great Communist Party than it is for its Cottolengo. Almost any well-informed person in Europe knows that for years after the Second World War the city's great Fiat works, with its tens of thousands of workers, was dominated by Communist shop stewards. But how many have heard of the Cottolengo?

I am not suggesting that the Cottolengo has failed. Tens of thousands have good cause to be grateful to it. Turin and the world at large would be an immensely poorer place without it. Those who labour there, and others who do similar work elsewhere, have kept alight a flame which today is in danger of extinction.

But around the Cottolengo in its early days there grew up an industrial society which was ugly and unjust. Its values were wrong. Profits counted for more than people. The masses were degraded and oppressed. They turned their backs on charity, and under leaders who had abandoned the Faith of theirfathers they drifted away from the Church in which Christian charity originated and which was the natural custodian of both charity and justice. Instead they joined the fight for justice under the banner of Karl Marx.

The great Cottolengo stands as a monument of Christian charity. It stands also as a living proof that charity alone in the modern world is, regrettably, not enough. It must be accompanied by a concern at all levels of society for justice as well. In our modern-pagan age there is a conflict between the two. Where the one flourishes the other tends to wilt. But this need not be so. In Christian teaching they complement and, indeed, permeate each other.

The need of our 20th-century society is to find a practical synthesis of charity and justice. To my surprise I found it in the life of Don Orione and in the Orders he founded. I had expected to find an abundance of charity, but in the back of my mind there lurked a fear that I might find among his followers a disregard, if not an actual distrust, of the modern fight for social justice.

As I got to know Don Orione the man better, it seemed natural enough that he should have realised that charity must be buttressed by a concern for justice. For he was a natural rebel. That was why he prided himself upon the fact that something of the spirit of the Garibaldians lived on in him. It is why Ignazio Silone, when he wanted someone with whom he could compare him, could think only of Lenin. His personality was many-sided. He was the very soul of charity, yet he was a fighter too. He not only wept for the poor, he could smart with them under the injustices they endured and, like them, long to right them.

He had no illusions about people. His ability to sense and to bring out the enormous good which is in most people was almost uncanny. But he knew and sensed instinctively the evil in them as well. He did not think that, because the rich industrialists and noblemen poured money into his projects, the rich as a class could necessarily be expected, without prompting and without pressure, to provide their workpeople with a reasonable standard of life. Nor did he think that, because the poorest of the poor saw his charity at work and loved it, the poor as a class would necessarily be prepared patiently to wait for an age of universal charity to bring them the good life.

Most of us know the splendid Christian type who is utterly devoted to works of mercy, who spends every spare moment in the service of the sick and poor. We know, too, the opposite type: the man who specialises in the pursuit of Christian justice; he is active in his union branch, accepts responsibility in the factory as a shop steward and in what little time is left him attends study groups where man's inalienable rights are earnestly discussed. Both types are necessary. They appear as opposites, but in reality they are complementary to each other. Each helps in his own way to Christianise society. But the greatness—or part of the greatness—of Don Orione was that he embodied both. So do his religious Congregations today.

One of Don Orione's priests who is the rector of a big technical school with some 700 students at Berna-Mestre, Venice's factory area, told me that there they deliberately trained their boys to be able to take an active part in industrial and political life when they left school. Many of them became shop stewards and union leaders. Others were now prominent in local labour politics. It was early in my quest for Don Orione, and this aspect of their work was new to me.

"How," I asked him, "does this fit in with your founder's ideas on Christian charity?"

The rector was puzzled.

"But Don Orione introduced the very idea of technical schools of this type into Venice," he said. "He was always emphatic that workers should be paid a just wage and be given good conditions. If he were alive today he would most certainly approve of what we are doing. He could not bear bent backs and bowed heads. We believe that in teaching them to fight for their rights we are making them true sons of Don Orione."

But it is also true to say that whilst they are trained to stand up for themselves, they are taught to do it without becoming infected with the spirit of class-war. That is where the charity of Don Orione comes in. To seek for justice is one thing. To introduce hatred into the struggle is quite another. That is something which is absolutely alien to the spirit of unlimited charity which was the outstanding characteristic of Don Orione, and to the very rich fund of social teachings of the Church to which he belonged.

The fact is that it is the absence of Christian

charity in the fullest meaning of the word, which turns what should be a healthy, virile pursuit of the good society into a squalid class-war. Had the very concept of that charity not already been largely lost before the Industrial Revolution, the whole bitter story of the past century might have been very different. Marx's message of hatred would have fallen on deaf ears. Human nature being what it is, men would, in any case, have had to fight for their rights. But the whole spirit of the fight would have been different.

It was the abandonment of the Church's conception of (charity), accepted for centuries by all Christendom, which made the Industrial Revolution, and the new society it brought with it, so unchristian and squalid from the start. The effects live on to this day.

Equally, in the less ruthless, far more civilised Welfare State, the absence of that same conception of Christian charity explains why all the best efforts of our secular humanists disappoint the hopes of those whom they are intended to benefit. The modern State needs a soul. It is up to Christians to provide it.

There, I believe, lies the special contribution which men like the Sons of Divine Providence can make to our social thinking. For they provide an example which others can follow. More than that, they point the way to a Christian life which is enriched at every level.

That, too, is the unique contribution which Don Orione made to 20th-century life. For he was a man who went "beyond all the normal limits" of Christian charity which lesser men have to observe. His life underlined, and underlined again, the power of a robust, virile, all-pervasive love in an age in which 'charity' sounds cold and 'love' has come to be thought effeminate.

No one, I believe, has pointed the way forward more clearly than Don Luigi Orione, the son of the Pontecurone *sulli*, whose beatification cause was started within only a few years of his death and whose name is loved and revered wherever men learn of his life or see his work.

THE END